DATE DUE

MR 17 '97		
MY 29 '97		
DE 19 97		
OC		

DEMCO 38-296

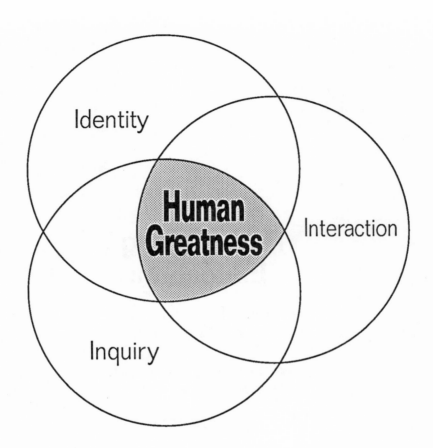

Identity

Interaction

Inquiry

Human Greatness

Redesigning Education:

A Guide for Developing
Human Greatness

by Lynn Stoddard

ZEPHYR PRESS

Redesigning Education:

A Guide for Developing Human Greatness

1988 The Great Brain Associates
1992 Zephyr Press, Tucson, AZ

ISBN 0-913705-64-0

Editor: Lisa Bowden
Cover Design: Michelle Gallardo
Design and Production: Richard Diffenderfer

ZEPHYR PRESS
P. O. Box 13448
Tucson, Arizona 85732-3448

Contents

Acknowledgments

T HIS BOOK IS DEDICATED TO MY GOOD FRIENDS MAX BERRYESSA, A RE-
tired professor of education at Brigham Young University, and
Charleen Cook, an outstanding first-grade teacher, who gave support
and encouragement when swimming against the mainstream seemed
like an impossible task.

I express deep gratitude to my sweetheart and eternal companion, Loraine, who retyped the manuscript countless times for me before I received a word processor from my children.

Finally, I wish to thankfully acknowledge my longtime friend Keith
Beery, a great researcher and program developer, whose brilliant work
has influenced much of the writing in this guide. The "faces" report
card, the parent priority surveys, and the full partnership concept
were patterned after materials that he developed. Beery developed a
process for helping people feel and show respect for one another—
ROSE, Respect for Others and Self-Evaluation—that is being used in
several school districts throughout the country.

Preface

IN 1972, AT THE PEAK OF THE BACK-TO-BASICS MOVEMENT, I WROTE AN essay that marked a turning point in my career as an educator. The essay grew from a personal dissatisfaction with what was happening in the school district where I was employed as an elementary school principal. The vigor with which I developed that writing project has carried me through a lifelong search for the meaning of "education," and has led to the creation of this book.

The essay was presented to the Utah Association for Supervision and Curriculum Development. It was written in response to the need for this organization to take a stand on vital issues and to restore vitality to the association. At the time, I had just finished a term as president of Utah ASCD and was state representative to the national board of directors. During those years, *Why Johnny Can't Read* by Rudolph Flesch had become a best seller and a great many Americans were won over by the belief that large doses of phonics were needed to rescue our country from illiteracy. The president and the U.S. Office of Education declared a national "right to read" effort; a large segment of our society became enamored with the notion that even babies could successfully be taught to read.

In the midst of this national rededication to reading, my paper appeared with the heretical title, "Learning to Read Should Not Be the Primary Purpose of Elementary Education." The paper suggested goals that could be more profitably pursued than reading and stated that teachers could more effectively foster the development of basic skills as well as other human qualities.

As the years went by, I was more and more troubled by the increasing number of students who were rebelling, both actively and passively, against the school system and turning to drugs, crime, and early sex. I was especially disturbed by my county's need for a new and larger jail.

The connection between the state of education and the rise in serious social problems haunted me for years until I arrived at some answers. Three major priorities for elementary education emerged from my deliberations:

▼ Help children develop their individual talents and feelings of worth as members of the human family;

▼ Help children develop the powers of expression and communication;

▼ Help children to develop their inquiring, creative minds.

In my essay, I talked about how reading and other subjects of the curriculum could be learned faster and with better results using what we now call a holistic approach. The success of the recent whole language movement is verification for a student-centered focus as a more effective way to help students learn how to read, for example, than is the archaic practice of toiling over the bits and pieces of phonics, word analysis, and syllabication. At the time, the essay sparked nothing more than a state debate on reading. In the end, the bits-and-pieces approach won out and Utah continued to support the industrial, standardized model of achievement.

My ideas have continued to grow and are reflected in the philosophy of this book, which captured the hearts and minds of the people in two elementary schools in Davis County, Utah, and provided them with the courage to go against the traditional curriculum-centered philosophy. I was inspired by the successes of the students, parents, and educators of Hill Field Elementary School and Whitesides Elementary School to resign from my position and write their story. The results of their experiment made me realize that we were onto something big.

Educating to develop human greatness is a vision that has finally been widely acknowledged; now is the time for that vision to take root and grow.

Overemphasis on the competitive system and premature specialization on the ground of immediate usefulness kills the spirit on which all cultural life depends, specialized knowledge included.

The competitive mentality prevails in schools and destroys feelings of human fraternity and cooperation. It conceives of achievement not as derived from the love for productive and thoughtful work, but as springing from personal ambition and fear of rejection.

The purpose of education is to nurture thoughtfulness. The lesser function of thinking is to solve problems and puzzles. The essential purpose is to decide for oneself what is of genuine value in life. And then to find the courage to take your own thoughts seriously.

— Albert Einstein

Overview

It is possible to design a system of education that will help individuals develop their full potential and realize their great worth to society while simultaneously reducing crime, teenage pregnancy, drug abuse, and suicide. My colleagues and I have developed, over a twenty-year period, a framework or pattern to follow in designing such a system. It is the result of teachers and parents from two elementary schools working together with a nontraditional approach.

This book will accomplish three things: first, it will show why traditional education has been so resistant to change — so reform proof — which must be understood before we can move ahead. Second, it will introduce a mental frame of reference that frees teachers and parents from slavery to obsolete traditions so that education can be redesigned. And third, it will give examples of strategies that can be used immediately with students to begin the process of building a totally new system of education.

Curriculum Worship: The Impenetrable Barrier

The decade of the 1980s was one of much talk about educational reform. In the name of reform, a few surface changes were made, but

This entire section originally appeared in the Spring 1990 issue of *Holistic Education Review* 3, no. 1 (Holistic Education Press, 39 Pearl St., Brandon, Vermont 05733-1007).

nothing really significant occurred to affect, deep down, what has been happening in schools for hundreds of years. Great teachers are still fighting the system in order to touch hearts and change lives, but more and more are burning out in the process. They find there is a limit to the energy they can give to overriding bureaucratic requirements, rules, and regulations in order to reach their students.

After studying and being involved in education for a combined total of nearly a hundred years, my colleagues and I believe that we have discovered the main barrier that prevents needed reform from taking place. It is a stubborn obstacle that will not be moved until we realize it is there.

The enormous dam that prevents progress in education is an attitude that is held by many educators — a belief that curriculum is king. Our society has an obsession with curriculum. Every few years another reform tide sweeps across the land and with it comes an irresistible urge to write a new curriculum in hope that this will cure our ailing system of education.

My associates and I have found that it is impossible to reform education within the prevailing frame of reference, which is characterized by a mental fixation on curriculum development instead of human development. Education has evolved into a purposeless organization that emphasizes standardized achievement and "minimum competence" over maximum achievement and the full development of individual potential. We have found in numerous surveys with groups of teachers and parents that they cannot name their state, district, or school goals of education. Those responsible for helping students learn do not know what the curriculum is supposed to accomplish. Thus, instead of being guided by goals, our teachers are slaves to curriculum, which has become an end in and of itself. All students are fed the same bland curriculum diet regardless of vast differences in gifts, talents, interests, and experiences. Teachers are required to do the impossible: standardize students.

An emphasis on standardization may be a major contributor to the alarming increase in suicide, teenage pregnancy, drug abuse, and crime. Students who do not fit the common mold into which they are being forced are dropping out of school in record numbers. Standardized achievement testing has become the trademark of the "effectiveness movement," through which a school's effectiveness is

6

> "To control and sort young people for the sake of institutional efficiency is to crush the human spirit."
>
> — Ron Miller

revealed to the bureaucrats who show their lack of trust by trying to control, through tests, everything teachers do. Neill and Medina, in an article in *Phi Delta Kappan,* show how standardized testing is "harmful to educational health":

> *When they are used as promotional gates, standardized tests can act as powerful devices to exclude groups . . . Minority students and those from low-income families are disproportionately affected. Research has shown that, when a student repeats a grade, the probability of that student dropping out prior to graduation increases by 20% to 40%. In other words, students who are not promoted because they have failed to reach arbitrary cutoff scores on often unreliable, invalid, and biased standardized tests are more likely to drop out of high school.[1]*

Perhaps the most serious consequence of trying to standardize and control everything teachers do can be seen in the huge deficit in human development. There are millions of brilliant, talented youths who have failed to develop their talents and gifts fully because our system of education is not organized to foster the personal development of individuals. When we aim for standardized achievement and minimum competence, we unknowingly and unintentionally rob each student of the full development of his or her unique potential, and we make nearly everyone feel cheated. The resulting loss of self-esteem often alienates students and causes them to withdraw from the mainstream and engage in drugs, early sex, and crime. Those who leave the school system feeling devoid of personal development — those who feel of least value — often choose to end their misery in suicide. All of this adds up to an incredible deficit in human development.

"If a man does not keep pace with his companions, perhaps it is because he hears a different drummer: Let him step to the music which he hears, however measured or far away."

— Henry David Thoreau

7

Breaking the Barrier: Education for Greatness

A plan that has proved effective in helping parents and teachers change their mental frame of reference about education is called *education for human greatness.* It hinges on a mental attitude best described by Marilyn King:

> *To accomplish any lofty goal, you must have a crystal clear image of that goal and keep it uppermost in your mind. We know that by maintaining that image, the "how-to" steps necessary for the realization of the goal will begin to emerge spontaneously. If you cannot imagine the goal, the "how-to" steps will never emerge, and you'll never do it. Clearly the first step to any achievement is to dare to imagine that you can do it.* [2]

King provides the key for breaking out of the curriculum trap. Education for human greatness consists of eight "frames" into which individuals can paint their own mental images of a new system of education.

Frame One
The Mission of Education

The first design frame is a mission statement designed to evoke a clear mental image that can be kept constantly in mind to act as a beacon:

Develop great human beings who are valuable contributors to society.

This mission represents a new definition for education: the process of becoming a valuable contributor to society, which relates to the Latin roots of educate, "educare," to draw out or bring forth greatness. If we put our minds to it, we can help every student develop a mental image of personal greatness. We have found in our work with teachers and students that even very young children can experience the joy of contributing to their family and school. The design frames that follow show that it is not difficult to help each child develop an identity of greatness, a mental picture of oneself helping the world become a better place, and realize that this is what it means to become educated.

Frame Two
Master Goals:
The Three Dimensions of Human Greatness

The second design frame consists of three specific master goals that further clarify the mission:

Identity: Individual talents and gifts, confidence, self-esteem, honesty, spirituality, character, and physical fitness.

Interaction: Compassion, love, respect, empathy, communication, and responsible citizenship.

Inquiry: Passion for learning; the ability to acquire, process, and use information to gain knowledge, create understanding, and solve problems.

These master goals are the result of years of trying to identify the qualities and characteristics that incline people to contribute to society. As my colleagues and I studied the lives of those who have made contributions throughout history, we have found three qualities that stand out: a strong sense of self-worth, deep feelings of love and respect for humankind, and an insatiable hunger for truth and knowledge.

These qualities, represented by the terms *identity, interaction,* and *inquiry,* are intended to be kept in mind as a crystal-clear vision to guide teaching and parenting. While teachers and parents may not be able to keep all elements of each dimension firmly in mind, they are able to concentrate on the three dimensions of human greatness.

These three dimensions offer a nontraditional frame of reference for education: they are people-oriented rather than curriculum-oriented. They help us to concentrate on human development — maximum individual achievement — instead of curriculum development with its twin brothers: minimum competence and standardized achievement.

9

The three dimensions provide a framework for redesigning education and allow us to escape from the curriculum trap and its confining, limited view of human potential.

The first dimension of human greatness, identity, probes the question Who am I? It describes the individual's most intense need, the need to be an important "somebody." One's identity is composed of all of the various elements of the self-image.

For a good many years in education we have been aware of the central role that self-image plays in our lives, as it governs all behavior. Each of us is always true to our self-image and behaves according to the kind of person we perceive ourselves to be.

"The great hope of society is in individual character."

— Channing

Feelings of worth can flourish only in an atmosphere where individual differences are appreciated, mistakes are tolerated, communication is open, and rules are flexible — the kind of atmosphere that is found in a nurturing family.

— Virginia Satir

Whenever we help a person elevate his or her self-image, we ourselves become contributors to society. In our work with students, parents, and teachers, we found that an effective way to raise self-image is to focus on a person's assets, which is in contrast to the traditional system that focuses on correcting inadequacies. Confidence and high self-esteem are the results when students discover what they can do well and strive to develop their unique talents and gifts. When we accept identity as the first dimension of human greatness and the primary goal of education, we begin to tap into the force that offers the greatest potential for growth: a person's self-image.

The second dimension of human greatness, interaction, answers the second most pressing need of people: the need to have healthy, warm relationships with others. It includes elements of compassion, love, respect, empathy, communication, and responsible citizenship. People who are lacking in this dimension often have difficulty keeping a job even though their level of skill and knowledge may be high. It is through positive interaction that many people make valuable contributions to society.

The third dimension, inquiry, describes another human drive — a hunger for truth and knowledge. The term *inquiry* in this context represents all that the human brain does to acquire, process, store,

and use information to build personal meaning and create new understanding. This term best describes how the human brain works.
Recent research on the nature of the brain indicates major changes
from the logical-sequential, imposed, test-based kind of instruction
that is the trademark of traditional education are in order. We have
. found that learning accelerates immensely when instruction is based
on personal inquiry.

Frame Three
E.T. Partnerships

The third design frame envisions parents and teachers working
together in a new kind of relationship:

Parents and teachers work *equally* and *together* to help students
grow in the three dimension of human greatness.

Traditionally we have viewed parents as subordinates to teachers.
They are people who go into school to help the teacher as "volunteers." With a change of mission for education, we see parents and
teachers working together as equals, performing their own special
functions, to help students grow in identity, interaction, and inquiry.

Frame Four
A Take-Charge Philosophy

The fourth frame returns control of education to students, parents, and teachers:

Teachers, parents, and students use curriculum as a means rather
than an end, as a servant rather than a master.

There is no need to develop more curricula. We are drowning in
workbooks, duplicated worksheets, and irrelevant textbooks — the
stuff that turns students off. The take-charge philosophy allows us to

turn to other sources for information: the real, here-and-now world of people, events, and interesting developments. It also solves another curriculum fixation problem that has plagued education for many years: the tendency to view each subject or course of study as a separate, isolated body of knowledge that is unrelated to anything else. Viewing curriculum as a means "puts Humpty Dumpty back together again" and integrates various disciplines into a unified whole. Money wasted on workbooks, textbooks, and worksheets could buy many microscopes, magnifying lenses, binoculars, scales, newspapers, library books, and other hands-on materials that invite self-initiated inquiry.

It is not curriculum that touches hearts and changes lives, but teachers and parents who are in tune with the drives of students: the drive to be important "somebodies," the drive for warm human relationships, and the drive for truth and knowledge. Students want the same things for themselves as we want for them. When we shift our focus from curriculum to students, we find that teachers and students are no longer the adversaries that they have been in traditional schools, but are now working together toward a common goal — the students' full development.

Frame Five
Evaluation of Greatness

The fifth design frame matches assessment procedures with what we are trying to accomplish:

Evaluation is used to assess student growth in greatness and for feedback and guidance.

New assessment procedures will evaluate what we are trying to accomplish: student growth in identity, interaction, and inquiry. Since in general these goals are not measurable with paper-and-pencil tests, we will need to turn to other evaluation techniques for feedback and guidance. We will look for manifestations of student growth in individual talents and gifts; self-initiated personal inquiry; and compassion, respect, and concern for others.

> "It is the whole child that we must nurture, not just one part of him. It takes a whole man or woman to live capably in our complex civilization."
>
> — Caroline Pratt

Frame Six
Multiple Intelligences

The sixth design frame helps us to form a mental image of each student as a unique individual:

Each person in the world is born with a unique set of intelligences to be developed, not a single IQ.

Howard Gardner and Joseph M. Walters have proposed a "theory of multiple intelligences" and have identified seven intelligences that are common to all human beings that vary in degree with each person. These are musical, bodily-kinesthetic, logical-mathematical, linguistic, spatial, interpersonal, and intrapersonal intelligences. [3]

Others have verified what we have known all along, that each person is a unique creation. Calvin W. Taylor has identified nine creative talents that are scattered unevenly across individuals, with each person possessing a unique profile of the nine talents. [4] Over twenty years ago, J. P. Guilford identified 120 different mental functions, for which IQ tests claim to measure no more than 8. [5]

Because of our traditional obsession with curricula, we have tended to ignore the work of those who reveal the individuality of human nature. A focus on people, instead of curricula, allows us to incorporate these valuable findings. To help each student nurture an individual identity of personal greatness, we must emphasize the discovery and development of each student's unique gifts and talents. The most important facet of a child's identity is his or her unique set of intelligences, and it is this human attribute that deserves our greatest attention. It appears that this part of human development is the most critical in determining whether a person will achieve the self-esteem and confidence necessary to reach his or her own potential.

Frame Seven
How the Brain Works

The seventh design frame gives us an updated view of how the brain works:

Humans learn through personal, self-initiated inquiry — the way they learned to talk and walk.

Brain research is telling us that logical-sequential, test-based instruction actually may interfere with learning. The workbooks, worksheets, and textbooks that are an integral part of the drill-test syndrome cause anxieties or boredom, which in turn causes human brains to shut down or to learn that schooling is irrelevant to life. We have found that a child will learn more through personal inquiry than through traditional methods that employ these dreary materials.

The work of Leslie A. Hart and Frank Smith have helped us to understand that it is an "insult to intelligence" to "teach" the brain how to think.[6] The brain thinks automatically, just as the heart beats and the lungs breathe. There is evidence that the brain files information according to the purpose for which it is to be used. This is the reason for the difficulty that so many people have remembering information they learn in order to pass tests. After the information has served its purpose, it is usually tossed into the brain's "dead" file. We are beginning to understand why test-oriented instruction seems to work for the short term but fails to produce long-lasting results. Brain research is helping us to better understand Plato's wise adage "Knowledge acquired under compulsion obtains no hold on the mind."

On the other hand, it appears that the brain handles information derived from self-initiated inquiry much differently. This information goes to the brain's "smelter," where it interacts with all previous and future input and is refined into the nuggets of personal meaning that are imbedded therein. We are beginning to grasp how we have grossly

14

underestimated the power of the human mind and how we can release great potential through an inquiry-centered approach.

"Greatness is a spiritual condition worthy to excite love, interest and admiration."

— Ibsen

Frame Eight
Strategies for Greatness

The eighth design frame gives us a place to invent and collect strategies that help students grow in the three dimensions of human greatness:

Strategies are the how-to steps that emerge when we hold a clear vision of our mission and goals in mind.

Over the years, many strategies have been created to help students grow in individual greatness. Many of these strategies are not welcomed within the traditional system of standardization. Others are embraced for a short period but are soon abandoned because teachers can't find enough time to fit them into the rigid, lock-step schedule, which points out the need for education to be redesigned completely from the bottom up.

The results of maintaining a clear mission were evident in our work at several schools; we watched students, teachers, and parents blossom with a burst of enthusiasm and creativity as they shed their preoccupation with curricula to focus on helping students develop the three dimensions of human greatness. When everyone concentrated on building identity, interaction, and inquiry, the school and indeed the entire community radiated a climate for creative inquiry. Many people became enthusiastic about inventing strategies for accomplishing the mission. The following are just a few examples.

The Great Brain Project

The first strategy that emerged was called the Great Brain Project. Students are invited to choose a topic of interest to them and study that topic in depth over a period of several weeks or months, trying to become a Great Brain — a "specialist," "expert," "mastermind," or "genius" until each student knows more about the topic than anyone else in the school, including teachers. When the student feels ready, he or she is encouraged to share this new knowledge with friends, relatives, and classmates through a carefully prepared Great Brain presentation that can include drawings, posters, charts, collections, demonstrations, and other visual aids.

It is gratifying to see what happens when students are given freedom and assistance to learn, as Leslie Hart would say, "with the brakes off." We do not need achievement tests to find out what is being accomplished; nor would they serve any useful purpose, since students learn facts and ideas that benefit their own interests, abilities, and personal needs. Achievement is clearly evident in the results of self-initiated inquiry.

During the presentations we watched, students were more attentive listening to their peers than they were listening to their teachers. They also seemed to ask more and better questions of their fellow presenters than they did of their teachers.

As we worked with several schools to implement the project, we observed many students changing their behavior and attitudes toward school and learning. Teachers saw several unmotivated, alienated students become eager, cooperative learners as they studied self-selected topics and received recognition and praise from their peers for outstanding accomplishments. This was a major clue to the role that schools can play in preventing people from becoming burdens to society.

Challenge Education

Another strategy that gives the responsibility for learning to the student is a big brother to the Great Brain Project. It is a strategy for high school students called Challenge Education. This strategy, developed by Maurice Gibbons, is patterned after the Australian aboriginal walkabout in which the young adolescent native must prove that he or she is ready to accept the responsibilities of adulthood by passing a test of stamina, endurance, bravery, and skill. The young person ventures into the wild alone for an extended period. In the tribe, most of adolescence is spent preparing for the walkabout challenge.

In Gibbons's American equivalent of the walkabout, a high school student spends most of the high school years preparing to make an elaborate presentation to friends, relatives, and classmates to prove that he or she is ready to enter the adult world and be a valuable contributor to society.[7]

The School Post Office

When the teachers at Whitesides Elementary School made a commitment to help children grow in positive interaction, they stumbled onto an amazing strategy almost by accident. A group of students and their teacher decided to organize a postal system to encourage written communication within the school. They built a large, official-looking mailbox and placed it in the center of the school near the office. They then announced to the school that there would be daily pickup and delivery of mail within the school. It was deliberately planned that the School Post Office would make next-day deliveries so students could concentrate on sending one day and receiving the next.

The impact was dramatic. Perhaps the most gratifying outcome of the post office was finding that students learned to read and write without being formally taught analysis, phonics, spelling, punctuation, and decoding. Teaching came in the form of responses to student needs: How do you spell_____? How do you address a letter?

In education, as in anything else, we get what we aim for. If we aim for nothing, we get nothing. If we continue to aim for curriculum as an end in itself, we will get a copious amount of curriculum development. On the other hand, if we aim for human development, our efforts will be rewarded with a large increase in the number of healthy, active citizens in our society. As supporters of this type of education, we have seen enough change in the lives of children and youths to be confident that educating for human greatness works to help individuals develop to their fullest. When individuals feel good about themselves they lose the desire to take harmful drugs, commit crime, hurt others or themselves. We invite you, the reader, to join us in fostering human greatness; we just need to put our minds to it.

"He who cherishes a beautiful vision, a lofty ideal in his heart, will one day realize it."

— James Allen

Notes

1. D. Monty Neill and N. J. Medina, "Standardized Testing Harmful to Educational Health," *Kappan*, May 1989, 688.

2. Marilyn King, "Ordinary Olympians," *In Context* 18 (Winter 1988). Sequim, Wash.: North Olympic Living Lightly Association.

3. Howard Gardner, *Frames of Mind* (New York: Basic Books, 1976); and Howard Gardner and Joseph M. Walters, "The Development and Education of Intelligences," in *Essays on the Intellect* (Alexandria, Va.: Association for Supervision and Curriculum Development, 1985).

4. Calvin W. Taylor, "Cultivating Simultaneous Student Growth in Both Multiple Creative Talents and Knowledge," in *Systems and Models for Developing Programs for the Gifted and Talented*, edited by Joseph F. Renzulli (Mansfield, Conn.: Creative Learning Press, 1987).

5. J. P. Guilford, "Intellectual Factors of the Intellect," and Robert Wilson, "The Structure of Intellect," in *Productive Thinking in Education* (Washington, D.C.: National Educational Association, 1968).

6. Leslie A. Hart, *Human Brain and Human Learning* (New York: Longman, 1983).

7. Maurice Gibbons, "Walkabout," *Kappan*, May 1974, 596.

Frame One
The Mission of Education

IF WE COULD ERASE ALL OUR PRECONCEIVED NOTIONS ABOUT EDUCATION and begin a new educational program, what would it be like? Imagine that you are part of a task force whose job is to establish a new system of education for a world in turmoil that is quickly destroying itself. Where do you start?

Consider the theories, the foundation, upon which education will be based. A new framework needs a "mission" statement. What you are trying to accomplish must be clearly in mind, because without that image, the steps toward realizing your goal will never emerge.

Our mission statement grew out of analyzing numerous surveys to determine parent priorities for education: "The goal of education is to develop great human beings who are valuable contributors to society."

This statement equates greatness with being a contributor to society. It sets a new goal for education: guiding students toward becoming great human beings. This concept is the foundation upon which this guide has been based. It is one that even very young children can understand; they learn quickly what it means to help out in a family, a class, or a community. It is easy to help children see that education is a process of "becoming" a good, contributing human being. "Greatness" is a measure of one's contributions.

Education for Greatness
A Winning Attitude

THIS SCHOOL FOSTERS:

Identity: Individual talents and gifts, confidence, self-esteem, honesty, spirituality, character, and physical fitness.

Interaction: Compassion, love, respect, communication, and responsible citizenship.

Inquiry: Passion for learning; the ability to acquire, process, and use information to gain knowledge, create understanding, and solve problems.

You too can become a pioneer, an education trailblazer, and begin designing a better system of education. The first step is important because it gives shape to your whole framework, just as a magnificent building is supported by the shape of its foundation. Decide on a mission statement and announce it. Declare what you are trying to accomplish. Get input from everyone involved, make modifications, get commitments, and have a publicity campaign. Make sure everyone understands your mission for education. Often when a company is failing, the most effective action to take is to remind everyone what the purpose of the company is, remind them in what direction they should be putting their energies.

For an organization to have a clear mission that is understood by its members serves three important purposes: it attracts talented people who agree with the stated premise and believe they can make a contribution; it unifies into a cohesive force all members of the organization as a team; and it weeds out those who are at odds with the organization's ideals.

At Hill Field Elementary School we promoted our mission by announcing the results of parent priority surveys through public meetings, newsletters, individual conferences with parents, and displaying a large poster inside the main entrance to the school (see above).

Looking back, I feel much more could have been done, although our efforts in publicizing the mission statement did rally support and solidarity among students, teachers, and parents. At Whitesides School we made another sign for the front entrance, which read: "Through these portals pass the world's greatest students, parents, and teachers." A banner could have been hung across the front of the school that stated: "This is an education for greatness school."

Summary of Frame One

▼ Decide firmly and clearly what your student-centered educational goals are.

▼ Construct a mission statement for your family, school, or community.

▼ Declare the mission through posters, flyers, letters, and meetings.

Frame Two
The Three Dimensions of Human Greatness

IDENTITY IS THE FIRST DIMENSION OF HUMAN GREATNESS. CHANGE A person's self-image and you change that person's life. One's self-image governs behavior. Each of us acts according to the mental picture we have of ourselves as individuals.

Maxwell Maltz states in *Psycho-Cybernetics* that "the self-image becomes a golden key to living a better life because of two important discoveries":

1. *All your actions, feelings, behavior— even your abilities— are always consistent with this self-image. In short, one will "act like" the sort of person one conceives him/herself to be. Not only this, but one cannot act otherwise, in spite of conscious efforts or will power. The person who conceives him/ herself to be a "failure type person" will find some way to fail, in spite of good intentions or will power, even if opportunity is dumped in his/her lap.*

2. *The self-image can be changed. Numerous case histories have shown that one is never too young nor too old to change his or her self-image and thereby start to live a new life.*

Self-esteem is an important element of education and yet comparatively little effort has gone into exploring its many applications. Nurturing identity has become a vital aspect of our plan because the most important thing we can do is help children and youth find a clear image of their own personal greatness.

Many people in every community are devoted to community service, to volunteering in hospitals and convalescent centers, and to helping their neighbors. They are generous with their time in helping the poor and homeless; they are true to their self-image of feeling valuable, kind, and caring. On the other hand, many people who are in our crowded jails acted in ways that reflect a negative, low self-concept.

If we are to encourage participatory, productive behavior, we need to concentrate on raising self-esteem and make the development of student identity a number-one priority.

Identity is more than self-esteem. It comprises a cluster of qualities and characteristics that are revealed in the process of discovering one's own potential and virtue. By identifying and developing these individual gifts, talents, and strengths, one's *identity* of personal greatness emerges.

Interaction is the second dimension of human greatness. It includes the qualities necessary for positive human relationships. This dimension revolves around the concept of compassion, which includes kindness, respect, love, service, forgiveness, cooperation, and responsible citizenship. No matter how "educated" a person may be, he or she is lacking in some way if these qualities have not been developed. In other words, education is not complete unless it affects the heart as well as the mind. The ability to feel and express compassion is directly related to the development of a person's identity. The ability to *interact* successfully, to communicate with compassion, is another key element in the triad that composes human greatness.

Inquiry is the third dimension of human greatness. It comprises those traits that develop in us a passion for learning and an ability to acquire, process, and use information to gain knowledge, create understanding, and solve problems.

Autonomous inquiry and creative intelligence are attributes that distinguish human beings from animals. Our mind allows freedom of thought, making each of us responsible for our own thoughts and

"Good character is more to be praised than outstanding talent. Most talents are, to some extent, a gift. Good character, by contrast, is not given to us. We have to build it piece by piece — by thought, choice, courage and determination."

— John Luther

"Of all the beautiful truths pertaining to the soul which have been restored and brought to light in this age, none is more gladdening or fruitful of divine promise and confidence than this — that man is the master of thought, the molder of character, and the maker and shaper of condition, environment, and destiny."

— James Allen

actions. The human brain is magnificent; it can accomplish unbelievably difficult tasks when required to do so. This marvelously complex instrument knows how to synthesize information, a function as natural as beating is for the heart. We can decide what problems to solve and the mind will go to work as long as we concentrate on the desired goal.

When we aim to fully develop the powers of inquiry, along with identity and interaction, we greatly increase the possibility of students becoming fully functioning, healthy, happy human beings.

These elements — identity, interaction, and inquiry — include all the characteristics and qualities necessary to begin to reach one's potential. The integrity of our society depends on the strength of character of its people. Those who successfully develop the dimensions of greatness will be the most valuable citizens.

The Three Dimensions of Human Greatness

Identity

High self-esteem, confidence

Development of individual gifts, talents, and potential

Responsibility, self-discipline, self-reliance, honesty

Sense of the spiritual, humility

Health and fitness

_____

_____

_____

Interaction

Compassion, love, empathy

Respect, kindness, consideration for other people

Cooperation, healthy communication skills

Responsible citizenship

_____

_____

_____

_____

_____

Inquiry

Curiosity, zeal for learning

Ability to acquire, process, and use information

Ability to gain knowledge and foster understanding

Ability to solve problems successfully

_____

_____

_____

_____

Summary of Frame Two:

▼ A person becomes a competent participant in society when he/she is successful in the areas of self-concept (*identity*), communicating with compassion (*interaction*), and autonomous learning (*inquiry*).

▼ Becoming educated is the *process* of developing in all three areas of human greatness.

▼ Develop your own requisites for human greatness and add them the matrix.

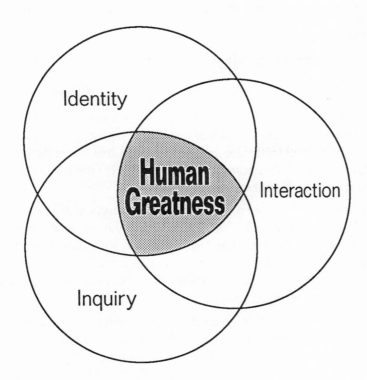

Frame Three
E.T. Partnerships

E.T. STANDS FOR *EQUAL* AND *TOGETHER*— AN UNPRECEDENTED FORM OF partnership wherein parents, teachers, and students are mutually responsible for helping the student grow in the three dimensions of human greatness. This common purpose unifies the group and makes the partnerships possible.

Partnership has been a buzzword in parent-teacher groups for years. It has represented a longing for cooperation between the home and the school. No one has been able to do much more than talk about it, and now we know why. It has been difficult for parents, teachers, and students to reconcile their varying points of view on and expectations of education.

In virtual isolation from each other, theoretically and practically, parents and teachers have operated in seperate realms. Parents send their children to school in the morning to be educated and teachers send them back in the evening believing that they have done their job. Since most parents are not trained to teach math, science, reading, etc., it has been disheartening for them to participate their child's education. In many homes, homework has become a nightmare because parents lose patience trying to help with work that seems irrelevant or difficult. Some students pit parent against teacher to avoid irksome tasks.

26

Cooperation in planning education is possible. By viewing curriculum as a means rather than an end, emphasis is placed on the process of education — the process of becoming a decent human being. A new curriculum is needed, one that takes a holistic approach and integrates all courses of study. With parents and teachers cooperating, the results are worth the effort it takes to build the partnership. Student learning accelerates dramatically; all who are involved change their attitudes toward education.

How to Build E.T. Partnerships

E.T. partnerships are possible when all parties adopt a mission for which they are responsible; when goals are student-centered, not curriculum-centered. Everyone must agree to share in accomplishing the goals by investing time, effort, and money.

The goals must be such that:

▼ they reflect the intentions of the group so all parties enthusiastically embrace them;

▼ they are presented clearly so all parties can keep them in mind and stay focused; and

▼ they are organized in a fashion whereby each partner's special role is defined and achievable.

Our mission — to develop the potential for greatness in students so that they may contribute positively to society — reflects the desires of my school at the time this program was developed, is clearly stated, and has defined roles and expectations for all parties involved. We have found that when responsibilities are shared and the goals are kept in mind, a feeling of solidarity and enthusiasm spreads among the partners.

What follows is a description of how this plan was implemented in the Hill Field Elementary School in Layton, Utah. It is offered as a pattern for the reader to modify to his/her own needs.

First Steps

In a workshop held one week prior to the opening of school, teachers mulled over the idea of how to expedite the process of getting to know students and their parents. The teachers decided that the traditional back-to-school night or open house had not been very successful in accomplishing their goals. First, they wanted to know the parents' expectations of the school; second, they needed to know about any special needs of each child; and third, they wanted to find out if there was any interest in teacher-parent team relationships. One or two hours of random intermingling or perhaps a teacher presentation had generally proved ineffective.

The Idea

At this point, it was suggested that each teacher hold a "partnership" conference with the parents of every child, as soon as the school year began. After much discussion, it was decided that teachers should be released from teaching during the second week of school in order to hold partnership conferences.

Operation

When the idea was presented to the Organization of Parents and Teachers, the officers were fully supportive. They agreed to furnish parent volunteers to monitor the classes while teachers attended a conference with each student's parents. At each grade level, a teacher was freed for conferences for three or four half days while a parent-volunteer supervised the classwork that had been planned by the teacher. The remaining teachers from that grade level provided support services to the substitute. High school seniors, who were taking child development classes, were also used. They were organized in pairs and for a half day handled the job as well as many parents.

At the end of the week of conferences, everyone was convinced that we were on to something big — a bridge had been built across the chasm that separated the school from the homes. Both teachers and parents expressed strong feelings of satisfaction and accomplishment from the experience. The school learned about parent expectations and the special needs of each child, but most important, a warm, working relationship was developed between the parents and teachers. Barriers of suspicion and mistrust were broken down when parents saw the teachers as fellow human beings whom they could help.

Some enduring friendships resulted from the partnership conferences. A poll revealed that, in terms of benefiting the children, 96 percent of the parents favored the early partnership conferences over the traditional back-to-school night or open house. An evaluation survey revealed the prevalent feelings among parents and teachers. Parents said:

"Make sure you continue to have these sharing sessions!"

"I just want to add that I really like the partnership conference. It's great to meet with the child's teacher right away and establish good communication. I also appreciate the opportunity to let the teacher know about my child— his talents, abilities, hobbies, areas that might need improvement."

"I always felt that back-to-school night did not really accomplish much. I think partnership conferences are a great way to start the school year!"

Teachers were equally positive:

"The conference gave me a head start with any behavioral or physical problems the child might have."

"It informed me of weaknesses and strengths at the beginning of the year."

"The partnership conferences helped me understand each child's special needs and fears, as well as each parent's hopes and concerns.

"This enabled me to plan ahead, trying to meet the children's special talents and problems in a positive way."

"Helps teachers and parents to know one another and work better with the child. The conferences give a feeling of friendship between parent, teacher, and child."

"A conference breaks the ice between parent and teacher. It removes the stranger feeling between them."

It appeared that parents had been waiting for a chance to have a voice in the education of their children. Most expressed appreciation for this opportunity. The parents who volunteered to monitor classwork while the teachers held conferences came away with a new appreciation for teaching. Several expressed, "We don't know how teachers ever do it day after day."

One of the greatest advantages of early planning was not immediately evident. Later in November, when administrators scheduled parent-teacher conferences for reporting pupil progress, there was no time wasted in getting acquainted. Communication had been flowing back and forth throughout the whole quarter.

Perhaps the most rewarding discovery was that teachers could now ask parents, How are we doing with the goals that were set in early September? How are you coming with your part? and, How do you feel I am coming with my part? Some of the teachers had found a way to set common goals with parents and share responsibility for accomplishing them. The conference soon became a planning session for the next steps in a united home-school effort.

A Pleasant Surprise

Many parents were caught off guard when they were invited to have a voice in their child's education and didn't know how to respond. They were accustomed to the role of subordinate who listened while teachers did most of the talking. It was a pleasant surprise for parents to be treated as equals who had knowledge to share. It was exciting for parents to be treated as "experts" who had information the teacher needed in order to do a better job. At the same time, some parents had considerable difficulty reversing those traditional roles and were overwhelmed with the challenge.

To address this problem, teachers asked parents to fill out a priorities survey that would reflect what they thought should be the goals of education for their child. They were also asked to fill out a talents and gifts (identity) profile. These activities were designed to help parents answer the questions that were to be discussed in the conference.

These questions appeared in a note that was sent to all parents:

Dear Parents,

You are invited to meet alone with me next week so we can make plans for this school year. This is intended to be a partnership conference where you and I can get acquainted and begin to build a trusting relationship as well as support each other in the important task of educating your child.

In preparation for your visit, please give some thought to these questions:

1. What would you like the school to accomplish for your child this year?

2. What are your child's special talents, gifts, interests, abilities, and needs that should be kept in mind?

3. How can we work together to acomplish these goals?

To assist you in these questions, please fill out the two attached forms and return them to me prior to the conference.

I hope you see this as an opportunity to share your voice and become more involved in the education of your child.

Sincerely,

The forms to accompany the note are as follows:

Priorities

for the education of _____
                                                    student

for the_____ school year

Please rate the following educational goals 1 through 10, according to your child's needs, in terms of what you feel is most to least important for the school to help you accomplish:

___ **Health and Physical Development**

Nutrition habits; physical fitness; strength, endurance, agility, and skill in sports, games, and life activities.

___ **Human Relations and Communication**

Getting along with others, leadership, cooperation, courtesy, respect, listening, speaking, reading, and writing.

___ **Identity and Individuality**

Self-esteem, self-confidence, self-discipline, responsibility, moral character, and the development of individual talents, gifts, interests, and abilities.

___ **Inquiry, Thinking, Learning**

Curiosity, eagerness to learn, study skills and habits, problem solving, creativity, and decision making.

___ **Science and Math**

Knowledge and skill in mathematics and the physical sciences.

___ **Arts**

Knowledge, skill, and appreciation for literature, music, dance, and the visual and performing arts.

___ **Work**

Initiative, self-motivation, self-direction, persistence, following through, and evaluating work; understanding of attitudes, knowledge, and abilities needed for various vocations.

___ **Responsible Citizenship**

Respect for and understanding of the workings of a democracy, appreciation for political processes and free enterprise.

___ **Environment**

Respect and maintenance of personal and public property, enjoying and protecting nature.

___ **Other** (describe): _____

_____

Individual Identity Profile

For _____

| Name | Grade | Date | Submitted by |

Please rate your child's strengths in the following areas using the 0-5 scale provided, with 5 as the highest rating.

	0	1	2	3	4	5

Linguistic Intelligence
- Verbose — enjoys talking and playing with words
- Enjoys writing, is fluent and expressive
- Reads a lot for pleasure and information

Musical Intelligence
- Sings, hums, whistles a lot (on key)
- Enjoys listening to a variety of music, notices various sounds
- "Plays" instruments, makes sounds, feels rhythms

Logical-Mathematical Intelligence
- Curious, asks many questions
- Collects, counts, compares, sorts, categorizes, and studies things
- Plays with numbers, enjoys arithmetic "problems"

Spatial Intelligence
- Remembers landmarks, places visited
- Knows directions, can draw and follow maps
- Enjoys and is good at drawing, painting, sculpting
- Is clean, neat, orderly

Bodily-Kinesthetic Intelligence
- Graceful, agile use of body
- Expressive with dance, gymnastics, gestures, mime, athletics
- Handles objects skillfully, can fix things

Personal Intelligence
- Understands and likes self, controls emotions
- Self-confident, plans, organizes, uses initiative, persistence, work
- Honesty and integrity, zest for life, thankful, appreciative

Social Intelligence
- Kind, friendly, loving, caring, generous, courteous
- Leadership/followership
- Listens attentively, demonstrates empathy/respect
- Is sensitive to others' feelings

General Intelligence
- Creative, inventive, imaginative
- Sense of humor
- Money management/thrift
- Hobby or expertise in a particular field of knowledge

Information on the *Priorities* and *Identity Profile* sheets were used as a basis for discussion in the partnership conferences. These surveys helped parents think about the needs and talents of their children and also made them aware of the fact that they had information that would improve the quality of education in their school.

When all the data from the *Priority* surveys was compiled, the most important goals of education came under the categories of identity, interaction, and inquiry. The *Identity* profiles reinforced the idea that every person is unique and talented in some way. Teachers were surprised to learn that children in third, fourth, fifth, and sixth grades, who also participated in the survey, had higher opinions of themselves than did their parents.

Another type of *Priorities* survey that reinforces education as a joint enterprise is shown on the next two pages.

Parent Priorities

for the education of _____

for the _____ school year

Responsibility, Where?
(check appropriate column)

(Complete left column first)

Priority 1, 2, 3, etc.

(most important to least important)

	All home	Mostly home, partly school	Mostly school, partly home	All school	Best done by school & home, working together
The Student Values Learning Is curious, accepts challenges, becomes absorbed, enjoys learning.					
The Student Values Work Takes initiative, is self-motivated, follows directions, plans and organizes, assumes responsibility, follows through, evaluates work.					
Self-Esteem Is aware of strengths and weaknesses, feels valuable and unique, feels comfortable when alone as well as in a group, trusts with discretion.					
Respects Environment Respects and maintains personal and public property, enjoys and protects nature.					
Respects Others Respects the rights, feelings, attitudes, cultures, and occupations of others; works cooperatively and enjoys other people.					
Reading Enjoys reading, is acquiring new skills.					
Written Communication Is acquiring new writing and spelling skills, enjoys creative writing.					

continued next page

Parent Priorities *continued*

Responsibility, Where?

(check appropriate column)

Priority	All home	Mostly home, partly school	Mostly school, partly home	All school	Best done by school & home, working together
Oral Communication — Listens and understands, can follow directions, enjoys and participates in group discussions.					
Mathematics — Enjoys mathematics; is acquiring new skills and concepts and is able to apply them.					
Physical Health and Development — Eats, sleeps, and dresses properly, practices personal hygiene, is developing new physical skills and strength.					
Appreciation of the Arts — Enjoys literature, music, visual and performing art.					
Student Individuality — The student is developing individual talents, interests, skills, and abilities.					
Responsible Citizenship — The student is developing appreciation for and understanding of the workings of a democracy.					
Other (describe): _____ _____ _____ _____					

These surveys were used in several schools in a number of districts, and they consistently produced very similar results. The surveys revealed, again, that the categories pertaining to identity, interaction, and inquiry were the top priorities of parents.

Partnership Meetings

As in any successful business, it is important for involved members to organize time to meet — one on one, in small groups, and in large groups — for evaluation and planning purposes. Meetings can be initiated by a parent, a student, or a teacher. They can be held day or night, at school, in a home, or at any convenient location. It is critical that teachers be released from working with students full time so they can spend time planning with parents. The ultimate aim is for teachers to spend one full day a week holding various kinds of partnership meetings with parents and students and for the remainder of the week to work directly with students. On partnership planning day, students can work on projects at home, in school, in the community, or in libraries.

Partnership meetings should always focus on designing new ways to help students grow and improve, as well as improving individual evaluation methods. A secondary priority is to improve the partnership.

Summary for Frame Three:

▼ Surveys can be used to evaluate educational concerns. The most common priorities include identity, inquiry, and interaction. These student-centered goals make E.T. Partnerships possible.

▼ Parents, teachers, and students working together in a full partnership and aiming for common goals can accomplish much more as a unified group than as individuals working alone.

▼ Partnership meetings are crucial for maintaining communication and should focus on improving ways to nurture the individual potential in every student.

Frame Four
A Take-Charge Philosophy

A T THE CORE OF *REDESIGNING EDUCATION FOR HUMAN GREATNESS* IS A creative, positive, holistic approach to education. It is based on a philosophy that differs from the philosophy of traditional education in that it is driven by goals rather than curricula. In traditional education, curriculum dominates the thinking and planning of teachers.

"If you know where you want to go, you have a much better chance of getting there."

— Anonymous

Maxwell Odiorne in *Management and the Activity Trap*, states: "Most people get caught in the Activity Trap! They become so enmeshed in activity they lose sight of why they are doing it, and the activity becomes a false goal, an end in itself."

Substitute the word *curriculum* for *activity* and you can see why traditional education lacks purpose and direction. Teachers often go through the motions of teaching the various subjects of the curriculum — reading, writing, arithmetic, etc.—as false goals, ends in themselves, because they often do not have an overall purpose clearly in mind.

Another falsehood sustained by the guise of the curriculum-god of traditional instruction is the so-called efficacy of letter-grade report cards and standardized achievement tests. These systems of measuring and reporting actually limit a teacher's ability to evaluate accurately.

According to Ron Brandt in his article called "The Search for Solutions," "U.S. schools use more standardized tests than schools in other countries, yet the vast majority of teachers and principals who devote hours to preparing for, giving, and interpreting the tests distrust them. They see increasing evidence that the testing tail is wagging the curriculum dog. They feel they are teaching — or would like to teach — much that is not tested. And they are weary of being compared — and having children compared — in ways they consider destructive."

A recent Rand Corporation study finds that "teaching behaviors that increase student performance on standardized tests is different from — in some cases the opposite of — teaching behaviors that increase complex cognitive learning, problem-solving skills, and creativity" (Dronka 1984).

The Great Brain Robbery

The long-standing practice of teaching only what is thought to be measurable has destroyed self-esteem on a grand scale and has prevented millions of students from developing to their fullest potential. IQ tests, in attempting to measure only four or five out of more than one hundred and forty identified mental functions, according to Guilford and Wilson (1968), have given a multitude of people the false impression that they are mentally inferior. These tests, as well as standardized achievement tests, are concerned with only a small portion of many logical, mathematical, and linguistic aptitudes. They leave untouched the musical, artistic, creative, mechanical, spatial, and kinesthetic areas of intelligence. Those who exhibit brilliance in areas outside the narrow confines of the common tests and grading practices have little chance for recognition or support. Generally, those unique talents are left undeveloped. IQ tests, letter-grade report cards, standardized achievement tests, and many textbook materials, including workbooks and worksheets, dominate instruction to the point that they, in effect, rob students of the opportunity to fully develop those talents.

The repercussions of maintaining these staid and restrictive practices are manifest in a tidal wave of social problems. Recent so-called reforms have only exacerbated the problem because they are virtually all linked to the measurable-curriculum philosophy. Teachers are asked to try a little harder, to push more buttons, but the wrong buttons are still being pushed; issues are not being addressed.

But the winds of real change are beginning to blow. Our nation's business leaders, in a comprehensive study of education, have submitted guidelines for reform in a report called "Investing in Our Children" (Committee for Economic Development, 1985). The authors call for schools to implement programs that develop traditionally immeasurable skills such as creative thinking, problem solving, honesty, dependability, self-discipline, learning skills, cooperativeness, hard work, and character.

Following is a condensed version of ten imperatives this committee listed for guiding reform of public schools:

The Ten Imperatives for Public Schools

1. Educational priorities should be better defined, and resources should be invested where the payoffs are high.
2. Employability should not be confused with vocationalism. Employability requires problem-solving skills, command of the English language, self-discipline, and the ability to acquire and apply new knowledge.
3. The central purpose of education is to develop the potential of every student, regardless of race, sex, or physical handicap.
4. Teachers are professionals. They should be held to high standards and rewarded accordingly.
5. Parents are a critical component of successful public schools.
6. Greater trust should be placed in the initiative of individual schools. Teachers and administrators should have increased decision-making power.
7. States should refrain from excessive regulation, centralization, and control of the schools.
8. A new coalition to support the public schools is needed — one that joins business, labor, and civic leaders with parents, educators, and school boards.

9. Education research and development and its effective utilization should be given greater emphasis.

10. Business should make a long-term commitment to support the public schools.

A Positive View of People

An essential part of the take-charge philosophy is a positive view of every human being. It is the magic touch of great parents and teachers that influences children and youth. It is the mighty force that helps students believe in themselves and overcome the crippling effects of low self-concept. When teachers and parents believe that students are talented and capable, the students begin to act accordingly.

Exhibiting a positive attitude can bring out the best in people. It comes easily once we understand the extraordinary nature of people and their unlimited potential.

What makes us tick? Is there a force in the universe that energizes people and makes us go? Who are we? Why are we here? Where are we going? Thinking about answers to these questions gives us a higher, positive view of people.

Two Sides of Humanity

As we carefully examine ourselves, we discover a dual nature. On the one hand, every person is unique and different. On the other hand, the heart, mind, and soul are energized by three common forces. The first force is the built-in drive for greatness, the hunger for *identity*. The second motivating force is the drive for affection and companionship. The need to love and be loved may be the most powerful force in human nature. It is the drive for positive *interaction*. The third force is the drive for truth and knowledge. The human brain is a magnificent instrument of curiosity; it is not a passive sponge waiting to be fed. This is the driving force of learning — *inquiry*.

Education for greatness is in harmony with human nature. It seeks the same things students seek for themselves: identity, interaction, and inquiry. When students see teachers coming over to their side to help them achieve their goals, the atmosphere of antagonism, which is prevalent in many classrooms, disappears. Students and teachers

"To put away aimlessness and weakness, and to begin to think with purpose, is to enter the ranks of those strong ones who only recognize failure as one of the pathways to attainment; who make all conditions serve them, and who think strongly, attempt fearlessly, and accomplish masterfully."

— James Allen

41

are no longer adversaries but are working together toward a common goal.

This is in direct contrast to our traditional system of education that evolved from the schools of colonial America where the hickory stick was used freely. The hickory stick is gone, but the traditional system of compulsory education still employs a belief that people need to be enticed or coerced into learning. The system of credits, grades, assignments, and requirements, which tend to stifle learning, shows our lack of faith in human nature. If we want to encourage learning we must demonstrate a positive view of people. This positive attitude radiates from each of us to the degree that we understand human needs and make a commitment to help individuals meet those needs.

If he is indeed wise he does not bid you enter the house of his wisdom, but rather leads you to the threshold of your own mind.

— Kahlil Gibran

People want to grow. With this view, teaching is not an act of aggressive indoctrination. Teachers become mentors or coaches who support and guide rather than impose instruction. When the classroom environment becomes more positive, students will try to live up to the expectations of the important adults in their lives.

Summary for Frame Four:

▼ The take-charge philosophy of education provides personal, purposeful, and positive tools for overcoming the forces of a staid tradition. It is *personal* because it returns control of education to the individual student, his/her parents, and the teacher. It has *purpose* because these three people share a common mission and keep their goals constantly in mind to guide their behavior. It is *positive* because parents, teachers, and students all show a strong belief in people and their potential.

▼ The vast majority of human intelligences are not, as yet, measurable. When we attempt to build curriculum around measurable objectives we severely limit human growth to narrow, lower-level thinking and rob students of the full development of their unique selves.

▼ Every human being comes equipped with a built-in drive for greatness.

▼ You can help stop the "great brain robbery" by adopting a take-charge philosophy. This is an attitude that keeps human concerns at the core of education and sees curricula as a means to achieve goals.

Frame Five
Evaluation for Greatness

E DUCATION FOR GREATNESS ATTEMPTS TO ASSESS STUDENT GROWTH IN
the three areas outlined previously. While traditional education
tries to measure and compare students' growth in the various subjects
of the curriculum, this program is concerned about student progress
toward human goals.

Inasmuch as we are taking charge of curriculum and using it to
accomplish our goals, we reject the traditional letter-grade report card.
The following evaluation instrument is one possible design for a tool
to assess student growth. It has been used successfully by parents,
teachers, and intermediate-grade students who have embraced the
vision of E.T. partnerships for human greatness. It is presented as a
prototype that can be used in designing your own evaluation instruments. Since all members of the partnership team are responsible for
helping students grow in greatness, they are to periodically fill out
the evaluation form and use it in the partnership planning meetings.

This evaluation instrument is subjective — based largely on the
observations and opinions of the evaluator. In the student's case, it is
based on personal feelings about his/her own growth. For those who
object to the soundness of this method of evaluation, I point out that,
by and large, the so-called objectivity of traditional letter-grade report
cards and standardized achievement tests is a myth. Most tests are

44

An Assessment of Student Growth in the
Three Dimensions of Human Greatness

Date _____ Evaluation for _____

Please indicate how much you feel this child is growing in each of the categories listed below:

Identity   Comments:

1. Self-esteem, self-respect, and self-confidence

2. Sense of responsibility for his/her own learning and behavior

3. Awareness and development of his/her unique strengths, talents, gifts, interests, and abilities

Interaction

4. Kindness, trust, thoughtfulness, tolerance, and respect for others

5. Social attitudes and skills — the ability to listen with understanding, express ideas, and get along with others

6. Enjoyment and ability to express him/herself in writing

7. Responsible citizenship, understanding of the workings of the democratic process, respect for environment and laws

Inquiry

8. Enjoyment of learning

9. Enjoyment of school

10. Curiosity, initiative, self-direction, and independence in trying to learn

11. Studying and seeking information from a variety of sources

12. Ability and desire to read for recreation and personal growth

13. Ability and desire to use knowledge to create, invent, think, and solve problems

Signature of evaluator

unable to detect any but the lowest level learning. They are poor assessors of growth in knowledge, attitudes, and skills. Paper-and-pencil tests are, at best, mere indicators of student progress and, to be complete, must be accompanied by parents' and teachers' observations and opinions. Until more tests are developed to assess student growth in areas other than those traditionally measured, we will have to rely chiefly on observation.

The document on the next page can be used in determining how primary grade students see their progress in the various areas.

Summary for Frame Five:

▼ Inasmuch as evaluation instruments often steer instruction, it is important that we develop assessment procedures that match our goals.

▼ Until more objective measurement procedures are developed, we can confidently create and use devices that are based on observation of student behavior and personal feelings.

▼ The parent, teacher, and student are jointly responsible for nurturing student growth and, therefore, should all share in the evaluation process.

Directions:

The parent or teacher is to read each question orally to the student, who then draws a smiling face, a frowning face, or an "in-between face" to represent his/her feelings about the question. ☺ ☹ 😐

Identity:

Example Answers

1. Do you do a good job of learning? ☺

2. Are you good at some things? 😐

3. Does your teacher like you? ☺

4. Do your classmates like you? ☹

Inquiry:

1. Do you learn about the things you want to learn about in school? ☺

2. Do you ask a lot of questions in your class? ☹

3. Do you read outside of school? 😐

4. Do you like to figure things out by yourself? ☺

Interaction:

1. Do you get along with other students? ☹

2. How do you behave in school? 😐

3. Do other people listen to your ideas? ☹

4. Do you get along with your family? ☺

5. Do you like to write? ☺

_____
Name

Frame Six
Multiple Intelligences

"Everything, men, animals, trees, stars, we are all one substance involved in the same terrible struggle. What struggle? ...Turning matter into spirit."

Zorba scratched his head [and said,] "I've got a thick skull boss, I don't grasp these things easily. Ah, if only you could dance all that you've just said, then I'd understand... Or if you could tell me all that in a story, boss."

— Nikos Kazantzakis

MANY PRINCIPALS OF SCHOOLS AND STAFF SPEND ALL SUMMER DEVELOPing a new curriculum only to find in the fall that the wrong kids show up. This problem is one that teachers face at the beginning of every school year. Children do not correspond to the curriculum that is designed for them. It might work if we were training dogs or seals, which can be trained to act in a consistent way, but people are unpredictable because they have a rich variety of experiences and freedom of thought. No two people think or act exactly alike, so it is unproductive to give students a common curriculum. Still, each year millions of dollars and countless hours are spent trying to develop a core curriculum that tries to standardize students.

A recent idea that captured the fancy of many educators and parents is "mastery learning." It is based on the premise that every child can learn a skill or body of knowledge to a "mastery" level if the right kind of instruction is provided and the child is given the time he/she needs. With this proposition, some educators believe they have finally made a breakthrough — the individualization of teaching and learning. At first glance, it appears to be true — educators need only to match their teaching to each child's rate and style of learning. In theory, the idea sounds wonderful, but in practice, educators find that it is virtually impossible, even with computers, to match instruction with each child's unique background and very complex style of learning and be able to have the time required to spend with any size group of youngsters.

Closer inspection of the mastery learning concept reveals that it is merely an extension of the curriculum-centered philosophy and factory model of education. The mastery idea requires a recycling of students through each concept or skill to be learned as many times as needed to absorb the material or accomplish the skill. This model is based on external manipulation — one agent acting on another to produce learning. It views each student as a lump of raw material to be molded or shaped by external forces. It emphasizes "what is lacking," that is, the knowledge the student has not as yet acquired.

Education for human greatness operates from a different frame of reference. It builds on a student's body of knowledge, strengths, unique profile of intelligences, and background of experience, rather than spends time concentrating on a child's deficits, a practice that destroys confidence and self-esteem. The focus on a child's knowledge and strengths allows for the brain to construct complex circuitry so that new knowledge and skill can be acquired.

Ronald is a prime example. In elementary school, he frustrated his parents, teachers, and psychologists because they couldn't figure out why he made little progress in reading, writing, and math — far below his peers. He appeared to be bright but refused to work for any of his teachers. He was a loner who did not join the other children at recess for sports. It was predicted that by high school, Ronald's name would be added to the growing list of dropouts.

In ninth grade, something happened. A sensitive choral teacher discovered in Ronald his gifts in music and helped him develop those. Almost immediately Ronald began to show an interest in other school subjects as well as music. His report card reflected this interest and Ronald soon was getting A's and B's in subjects in which he normally received D's and F's. Ronald later starred in the high school musical production, sang with the prestigious a cappella choir, won a music scholarship to college, and became a star performer with the Weber State Singers.

Ronald may never have a career in music. The important thing to note is that his talents have been unlocked through music. By con-

"Whenever a kid isn't learning, experts are quick to conclude that the problem is a 'learning disability,' ...but they're never quite clear about *who has it!* Perhaps you've noticed that they *never* call it a '*teaching disability.*' The implication is always that the cause of the failure is the kid's brain is weak or damaged, often by presumed genetic causes."

— Richard Bandler

49

centrating on his strength, Ronald felt important and worthwhile. This focus on his musical talent helped Ronald make connections that helped him learn to read, write, and solve problems with mathematics. Prior to the discovery of Ronald's gift in music, he had been pushed through the three R's many times with sincere attempts to match instruction with his illusive learning style. The result of concentrating on curriculum instead of concentrating on Ronald was a reduction in self-esteem. His life changed because a great teacher was sensitive to his special talents. We can only wonder what might have happened if Ronald had been immersed in a system of education that valued individuality from the very beginning. Perhaps nine years of misery, loneliness, diffidence, and stagnation could have been avoided.

> "Understanding one's own magical mystery is one of the teacher's most important assets if he is to understand that everyone is thus differently equipped."
>
> — Buckminster Fuller

The Theory of Multiple Intelligences

Education for human greatness recognizes, indeed prizes, celebrates, and fosters individuality. The point is to promote a student's growth in his/her unique set of intelligences, talents, gifts, interests, strengths, and abilities. The identification and development of one's unique profile of intelligences is one of the main ingredients for developing identity. Understanding this profile helps a student build the confidence and self-esteem necessary to take risks in learning. This is one of the reasons why knowing oneself is the most important knowledge a person can possess.

We now know that it is not merely fingerprints that distinguish one person from another. It is everything from voice pattern to size, shape, location, and function of all body parts. Roger Williams, in his great book *You Are Extra-Ordinary,* writes:

> *The basic answer to the question, "Why are you an individual?" is that your body in every detail, including your entire nervous system and your brain (thinking apparatus), is highly distinctive. You are not built like anyone else...*
>
> *If we are trying by education and training to make people uniform, we are failing dismally. Every person continues to carry with him, as long as life lasts, a host of desires, tendencies, and attitudes that are an outgrowth of his own inborn, highly distinctive makeup and unique development. Millions*

have been ruined psychologically because of a failure to recognize this fact.

It is futile and damaging to try to force everybody into the same mold.

Howard Gardner and Joseph M. Walters have developed a theory of multiple intelligences, which ascribes to every human being a unique profile of intelligences. They propose that each person is equipped with his/her own set of the seven intelligences previously mentioned: musical, bodily-kinesthetic, logical-mathematical, linguistic, spatial, interpersonal, and intrapersonal.

The *Identity Profile* on page 33 was adapted from these seven intelligences to help identify a child's unique combination or blend of abilities that could be expanded. When we use this device we can begin to see possible directions for helping a child build on his/her strengths. The Great Brain and Shining Stars programs, described in Frame 8, are ways to help children discover their individual intelligences as they freely choose topics and areas of interest to study in depth.

It is important to provide as many avenues as possible for a child to identify and develop his/her unique profile of intelligences. The Shining Stars program may appeal to some youngsters who are not interested in the Great Brain program and vice versa. The fact that every person is unlike any other makes it imperative that we quit trying to make everyone alike with a common curriculum.

People who are gifted in one form of bodily-kinesthetic intelligence are sometimes labeled "dumb jocks." This is due to ignorance of the brilliant brain activity required for one to be talented in sports. Consider, for example, what the brain must do for a person to be talented in tennis.

At the moment the ball leaves the server's racket, the brain calculates approximately where it will land and where the racket will intercept it. This calculation includes the initial velocity of the ball, combined with an input for the progressive decrease in velocity and the effect of wind after the bounce of the ball. Simultaneously, muscle orders are given: not just once, but constantly with refined and updated information. The muscles must cooperate. A movement of the feet occurs, the

"If we do not find a place for the inventor, the unorthodox thinker, the investigator of a fresh line of inquiry, or the contemplative as opposed to the traditional doer, then the educational system will perpetuate only what already exists and society will stand still... as teachers we have a great responsibility for the survival of imagination. It can so easily get lost in childhood, and once imagination has been allowed to die, it is very difficult to restore."

— A. Yardley

51

racket is taken back, the face of the racket kept at a constant angle. Contact is made at a precise point that depends on whether the order was given to hit down the line or cross-court, an order not given until after a split-second analysis of the movement and balance of the opponent.

To return an average serve, you have about one second to do this. To hit the ball at all is remarkable and yet not uncommon. The truth is that everyone who inhabits a human body possesses a remarkable creation. (Gallwey, Inner Tennis*)*

The same kind of brilliant thinking required in tennis is necessary for a person to be gifted in basketball, soccer, football, or any sport.

Frank is another example of what can happen when a child's unique gifts are nurtured by the educational system. He was gifted physically, but in elementary school Frank's talents went largely unnoticed because the school placed great emphasis on the "basic skills" of reading, writing, and arithmetic and viewed physical education and recess mainly as rest and relaxation in between the serious business of "real learning." Frank performed poorly in the high-pressure academic program of his elementary school.

"We are shaped and fashioned by what we love."

— Goethe

Like Ronald, Frank's ability for learning the three R's was enhanced only after his teachers in junior high school began to recognize and reward his brilliant bodily-kinesthetic intelligence. He won the county wrestling championship for his weight and led the school basketball team to a first-place trophy. In high school, Frank received letters in four sports and was named the school's outstanding scholar-athlete by the end of his senior year, attaining a grade point average of 3.7.

Frank and Ronald are examples of what can happen when education becomes a process of nourishing individual intelligences. Schools and families can generate a great variety of experiences and activities that help children learn about themselves and become self-directed.

Williams said, "Young people need to learn to tune their lives to their own unique capabilities. Too often unattainable goals are sought while, through ignorance, real talents remain undeveloped, unnecessary frustrations arise, and personalities thus become distorted and twisted. Learning about one's own distinctiveness, and learning to value and respect the distinctiveness of others are fundamental to a real education."

It is estimated that in the labor force 80 percent of the people do not enjoy their jobs. When individuality is valued, we can begin to help each person develop a unique set of intelligences and find an occupation that matches his/her unique profile.

An individual's identity grows as that person develops his/her individual set of intelligences. Schools that provide a broad spectrum of opportunities for children to discover and develop their individuality help to foster their students' identities. With a program for human greatness, children are given many chances to try their wings in a great variety of endeavors. Parent partners spend as much time as they can at school and at home giving students a taste of everything from model building to knitting and weaving to electronics, kite building, marbles tournaments, jacks, checkers, and chess. Nothing is intentionally left out of the curriculum. We know a boy who was having difficulty learning to read but who, at the same time, was a genius on a unicycle. His unusual bodily-kinesthetic intelligence carried him through a time when he needed feelings of dignity and self-respect.

> If I force the child to see the world in the narrow patterns of my history and my perspectives, I lose the opportunity to be a true teacher.
>
> — Bob Samples

Roots

There comes a time in many individuals' lives when they want to find out about the people they are descended from. When children study the lives of their ancestors, they often discover that a particular gift or talent runs in the family. This new knowledge becomes part of the process of recognizing and building one's identity.

Parents can be important partners with teachers in helping students research old journals and records, interview grandparents, uncles, aunts, and visit genealogy libraries. "Roots" diagrams like the following can be filled out and the child can find out all he/she can about his/her parents, grandparents, or great grandparents.

Journals, letters, and family histories stored in attics and other out-of-the-way places become treasures in a search for one's roots. If some of these materials can be found, children may want to docu-

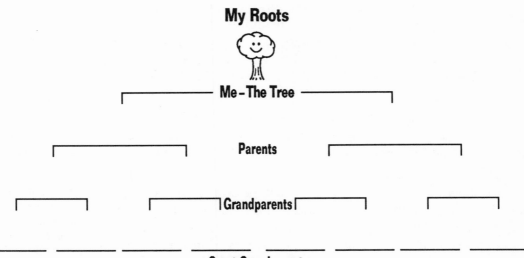

My Roots

Me – The Tree

Parents

Grandparents

Great Grandparents

ment their lives by keeping a journal. It gives dignity to a child to suggest that his or her life is important enough to document for posterity. Writing then becomes a tool for recording important ideas, events, thoughts, feelings, and aspirations.

The theory of multiple intelligences and the idea that every person has a unique profile of intelligences explain why so many discipline problems develop in a traditional school system that stresses conformity.

Summary for Frame Six:

▼ Human beings are born with unique sets of intelligences. People are more apt in some areas than in others.

▼ Developing one's identity means developing one's unique profile of intelligences.

▼ A school or home that concentrates on a child's strengths, acquired knowledge, and unique intelligences will facilitate and enhance that child's ability for learning.

▼ Helping a student identify and develop his/her own repertoire of intelligences boosts that person's self-esteem and enables him or her to make positive contributions to society.

▼ The Roots project is just one example of the kinds of programs that foster an identity of personal *greatness*.

Frame Seven
How the Brain Works

AS WE DESIGN A NEW SYSTEM OF EDUCATION, WE MUST BE SURE THAT IT is in harmony with the way the brain works. To do otherwise would be like speaking to someone in a language he or she does not understand.

Research shows that human brains are very different from animal brains — perhaps not so much in form as in function. Humans are endowed with freedom of thought and creative imagination, whereas animals are "programmed" to follow a prescribed course. This combination of freedom to think and creative power gives people amazing potential. Information entering the brain can be routed to any of a billion possible locations. Usually, the randomly supplied information is placed in the brain's "open file" for immediate retrieval.

Most teachers are familiar with the phenomenon of teaching students a concept, testing to find if it was "learned," and discovering later that many students act as though they never heard the information that the teacher tried so hard to convey. Many elementary school students are noted for their ability to learn spelling words in order to pass a test on Friday, and the next week , in a written composition, absolutely butcher some of the very same words from the test. This common occurrence verifies what brain research is showing. The brain usually stores information according to the purpose for which it

"The key to understanding how people interact in their environment may be in knowing how the brain works, what behavioral actions are coupled with specific brain functions and how brain processes can be assessed in educational institutions."

— Perone and Pulvino

was learned. Much of the learning in traditional systems of imposed instruction is for the purpose of passing the next test. Information is put into the brain's "closed file" as soon as the test is over because it has already served its purpose.

In addition to having open and closed "files," the human brain has a third file, which we will call the "smelter." This is where information obtained through personal inquiry is placed. This information is not merely "available," as in the open file, but it is ripe and ready to supply energy for the creative imagination. Knowledge acquired through personal inquiry is bubbling with energy to keep the brain thinking. Such knowledge obtains a hold on the mind and therefore changes attitudes and affects lives.

"The inquiry method is not designed to do what older environments try to do. It works you over in entirely different ways. It activates different senses, attitudes, and perceptions; it generates a different, bolder, and more potent kind of intelligence.... It will cause everything about education to change."

— Neil Postman and Charles Weingartner

Self-initiated, personal inquiry is the language of the brain — the only means whereby personal meaning is derived from thousands of pieces of information that flow into the brain each hour. That is why *inquiry* is the third dimension of human greatness. Parents and teachers must stop thinking of teaching as an act of delivering the same prescribed curricula to all students and devise ways to nourish personal inquiry so that more information can be placed in the smeltering vat to be refined and assimilated.

Leslie Hart, one of the country's foremost interpreters of brain research for education, gives another version of how the brain works and learns. His "Proster theory" asserts that the brain is an amazing instrument that detects patterns and notes similarities and differences in the millions of randomly supplied bits and pieces of information (including features and relationships) that continually enter the brain; it then assembles these pieces to form concepts and programs of action. This theory explains human behavior as a process of storing in the brain fixed sequences of actions that can be called forth as needed. Neve, Hart, and Thomas say:

> Brain compatible instruction dispenses with the hoary and ubiquitous notion that learning must occur in some arbitrary, sequential, 'logical' order that has been officially sanctioned. Brain based instruction stems from recognizing that the brain does not take logical steps down one path (like a digital computer) but can go down a hundred different paths simultaneously (like an enormously powerful analog computer). Ran-

dom learning, like assembling a complex jigsaw puzzle, is seen as the way human brains work. This is aided by many varied experiences and by a global emphasis rather than by splintering learning into narrow subjects or units.

These three ideas — first, that significant learning is based on personal inquiry; second, that the brain learns best by assembling randomly derived information; and third, that programs are built from action — suggest major changes for education. Since the brain can handle a great many pieces of information all at once, it is not necessary to learn item A before item B before item C. In fact, we probably inhibit learning when we try to determine for a child which pieces of information are lacking and, therefore, need to be learned according to an arbitrarily chosen sequence.

Everyone learns to walk and talk through a process of personal inquiry by assembling millions of bits and pieces of randomly supplied information. People learn to talk without formal instruction, so why should we be surprised to find many children learning to read on their own? We now know that *all* children learn to read *on their own*, with or without instruction. That is the way the brain works.

This is not to say that nothing can be done to assist the child in learning to talk, read, or write. Some children learn to talk before others because they are immersed in a talking environment. Parents and brothers and sisters in some families talk a great deal more with each other, and with the emerging child, than do members of other families. When there is a large quantity of pleasant conversation entering a child's brain he or she sees human language as desirable and soon begins to mimic those around him or her. On the other hand, if a child is raised in a home where there is very little pleasant talk, the child is often retarded in learning to communicate with language.

The same principle holds true for reading and writing. A child immersed in a reading and writing environment will learn these skills with little or no formal instruction, because the brain is given a chance to gather and assemble information and build programs of action on its own.

Frank Smith, a noted linguist, says:

Learning to read is a complex and delicate task in which almost all the rules, all the cues, and all the feedback can be obtained only through the act of reading itself. Children learn to read only by reading. *Therefore, the only way to facilitate their learning to read is to make reading easy for them. This means continuously making critical and insightful decisions — not forcing children to read for words when they are, or should be, reading for meaning; not forcing them to slow down when they should speed up; not requiring caution when they should be taking chances; not worrying about speech when the topic is reading; not discouraging errors...*

Respond to what the child is trying to do. *To my mind, this rule is basic. There is no alternative. The rule recognizes that the motivation and direction of learning to read can only come from the child and that learners must look for the knowledge and skills they need only in the process of reading. Learning to read is a problem for the child to solve.*

Brain research is now telling us that the best way to help children learn the skills of communication — listening, speaking, reading, and writing — is to immerse a child in a pleasant, interactive environment where he or she has as many opportunities as possible to actually practice these skills.

Just as a child can't learn to ride a bicycle until he or she gets on and starts pedaling and balancing, neither can a child learn to communicate until he/she engages in the art of real communication. A child learns to read by reading, to write by writing, to listen by listening, and to speak by speaking. The brain picks up the cues it needs while it is engaged in the process.

This means that we need to drastically reduce the amount of time we spend teaching reading, writing, and speaking and start having children spend more time actually doing these things. The traditional classroom with children seated in rows and raising hands for permission to talk must give way to a variety of settings where courteous, pleasant conversation is encouraged. We know of a school where the principal would not allow children to talk or even whisper in the lunchroom! What a great crime that is.

The School Post Office

When the teachers at Whitesides Elementary School made a commitment to help children grow in the second dimension of human greatness, interaction, they discovered an amazing tool. One group of students and their teacher decided to organize a postal system to encourage written communication. They built a large, official-looking mailbox and placed it in the center of the school. They then announced that they would make a daily pickup and delivery of mail within the school to the addresses written on the envelopes. Students, teachers, principal, parents, custodians, cooks, secretaries, and librarians were encouraged to write notes and letters. Students were given pointers on how to write letters that would build self-esteem (identity), show love and friendship (interaction), and encourage intellectual activity (inquiry). Children were encouraged to write not only to their close friends but to someone whom they felt needed a friend. They were also encouraged to write thank-you notes to cooks and custodians and to write concerns to the principal and student government officers.

The school post office made a dramatic impact on the life of the school. Within a day or two of its inauguration, many other school activities had to be drastically curtailed or set aside in order to provide students with the time they needed for writing. The flood of mail was so great that the students who started the project had to reorganize their room into a mail-processing center. Some adults in the school received so many letters that they became concerned about how they would have the time to answer them. Children started writing letters at home and rushing to school each day to read their mail.

Within two or three days, the teachers began to be concerned about the amount of time taken up by children writing letters. It was felt that the traditional subjects of the curriculum were starting to suffer as there was little time for formal instruction.

At this point the teachers came very close to returning to traditional, imposed instruction. Some thought they might lose control; students appeared to be learning to write, read, and spell without being "taught" except in response to individual children asking for specific help. Some teachers wanted to close down the post office because it interfered with their traditional role of planning and teaching specific, testable lessons. The inquiry process produced learning on so many levels that teachers were unable to keep track of it.

Fortunately, cooler heads prevailed. A few teachers who thrived on uncertainty suggested the staff should step back and look at what was happening. Weren't children writing as never before without being coaxed into doing so? Weren't they learning how to spell new words at a very rapid rate? Weren't kindergarten and first graders learning how to read and write? Weren't children learning how to address envelopes properly and discovering the importance of putting a return address on their mail? Weren't they learning the necessity of writing legibly?

The school decided to allow the post office to continue operating for a few more days to see what would happen. The quantity of written interaction was so profuse it appeared that the second dimension of greatness, *interaction*, was being developed at a very rapid rate. In addition, the third dimension, *inquiry*, was being exercised as students sought help with vocabulary, spelling, and grammar.

After about a week, post office fever subsided somewhat as some children concentrated on the quality of their letter writing rather than the quantity. Many children started to expand their contacts to include pen pals in other states and other countries. The teachers decided to keep the post office as a permanent part of the school and rotate the various jobs among the classes. Most classes made trips to the local post office to learn how to operate a mail delivery system.

The school post office is an experiment that is compatible with how the brain works and learns. It involves a flood of randomly supplied information, personal inquiry, and learning by doing. Perhaps most important, it is an activity that generates its own steam. Students do not need to be coaxed, assigned, or required to participate.

Great Brain research and the Shining Stars Talent program are also activities that are "brain compatible" and nourish student growth in each of the three dimensions of human greatness with emphasis on a particular dimension as shown in the following diagram:

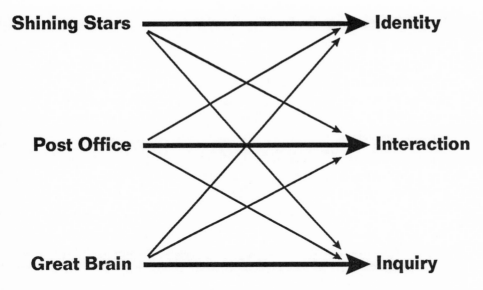

In the beginning stages of learning to read, children pick up the most useful information when parents and teachers read interesting material to them regularly. There is no substitute for a child seeing parents and teachers enjoying reading and participating with them in the process. There is a special kind of bonding that occurs between loved ones when a young child enjoys a book with parents or grandparents.

Teachers and Parents as Models

To provide the kind of climate where great brains can operate full steam ahead, schools need to shift from imposed, logical-sequential instruction with a uniform curriculum for everyone to a program that revolves around personal inquiry. Parents and teachers can do this by making sure that the primary goals steer the ship. We must shift from the traditional role of "knowledge dispenser" to that of model, mentor, and organizer of experiences that help students grow.

It is important to make sure our children see us doing the things we want them to do. If we want a child to read, we must read; if we want a child to be a curious investigator of the world, we must show him/her that this is important; if we want a child to love, we must love; if we want a child to be honest, we must demonstrate personal integrity.

Inquiry Centers

Schools and homes can become inquiry centers where objects from nature, for example, are collected and examined with magnifying lenses, microscopes, and scales, and where materials for drawing and painting are available (the best way to examine an object is to draw or paint it), as well as books and articles about the objects, and writing materials.

Ample money for science equipment and reference books can be found by shifting funds normally spent on textbooks, workbooks, and ditto sheets into funds for materials that invite personal inquiry.

Old and new elementary school science books, issues of *National Geographic*, and other magazines can be separated and re-bound into individual, single-topic study units. Newspaper and magazine articles can be collected and assembled into files on a great many different subjects.

Inquiry Excursions

Every community has a plethora of interesting places to investigate. Just step outside and start looking, listening, smelling, and touching, and you will discover living and nonliving things you never knew existed. If we take children on our excursions, they will soon get caught up in the exciting adventure of the "great brain business." I know an outstanding naturalist in our area who gets down on hands and knees with a hand-held magnifying lens and takes his students on "nature creeps" to introduce them to the bustling miniature world under our feet.

Meaningful Math

A great many people in the world today have trouble with arithmetic because they were taught this subject as a goal and end in itself — a set of processes learned for filing in the "dead file" after passing the tests. We have seen hundreds of first and second graders mentally crippled by math workbooks and worksheets that are supposedly designed to teach math processes. What often happens is that the student learns the pattern of a mathematical operation and memorizes it so that it appears that he or she is learning arithmetic. In

> "There is *so* much more inside our minds than we suspect. There is *so* much more outside than we are capable of being curious about. It's only that growing sense of curiosity that allows you to capture the enthusiasm that makes even the most mundane or the most fascinating task worthwhile, fun, and intriguing."
>
> — Richard Bandler

reality the child who becomes good at workbook and textbook math is often incapable of thinking with numbers and of solving even the simplest of real-life, practical math problems.

The solution to this problem is to spend the workbook budget on magnifying lenses, weights and measuring devices, and other hands-on math materials to guide the child into counting, comparing, weighing, and measuring the objects and events of the child's real world. A child will learn to think numerically only when he or she is engaged in personal inquiry. Some examples:

Divide children into small groups (three to five people). Give each group an assortment of rocks of various sizes, shapes, weights, and colors. Challenge the children to classify the rocks into as many possible categories as they can. Invite them to arrange the rocks from lightest to heaviest. They should be ready to prove their solution. (Weighing devices can be invented by the students.) Have them arrange the rocks from smallest to largest and prove their solution. (Measuring devices can be invented by the students.)

If the school or home is near a highway, invite children to do a traffic study to determine: How many vehicles pass by in one minute? In ten minutes? One hour? One day? How many different kinds of vehicles use the highway? Which kind uses it the most? The least? On the average? Challenge students to invent procedures for measuring how fast each vehicle is traveling. (Think safety on this one.) What is the average speed? (Why do so many people ignore the speed limit?)

How many apple trees can be expected to grow from the seeds of one apple? One pumpkin? One watermelon?

Which child in the classroom is tallest? Shortest? By how many inches is the tallest student taller than the shortest student? Whose heart beats the fastest? Slowest? After exercise? Resting? Why?

Get the idea? You can easily break through the constraints posed by workbooks and textbooks and help students learn about math by looking into the unlimited opportunities all around us. Mathematical reasoning learned from personal inquiry is the only kind that lasts. Most Great Brain projects are loaded with real problems to be solved. Try to save textbook and workbook math as a last resort since its effectiveness is not as long lasting.

Art, Music, Drama, Dance

The arts are areas that provide the five conditions of brain-compatible education — magnetic appeal, random input, personal inquiry, learning by doing, and free choice. Wise parents and teachers will make sure that materials are available and time is provided for students to explore these areas. Mentors will also expose children regularly to great art, music, dance, and drama and help them acquire an appreciation for beauty.

A Living Curriculum

Since brain-compatible education requires learning by doing, students can learn about democracy and the free enterprise system by involving themselves in school government and establishing small businesses.

Industrial Arts

Many students are gifted with manual dexterity; they are good at fixing, assembling and disassembling, building, designing, and constructing things. If we do not provide for the growth of these intelligences, we will deprive our society of a valuable human resource. Provide space, materials, and time for students to invent, create, and fix things.

Goal-oriented parenting and teaching results in the kind of environment that is necessary for the great brain business to occur. In other words, if we constantly focus on helping students acquire the dimensions of greatness, we will also be providing the five conditions necessary for brain compatible learning.

Summary for Frame Seven:

▼ Freedom of thought and creative imagination make human beings unlimited in their potential.

▼ Much learning that is derived from traditional, logical-sequential, imposed instruction is filed in the brain's closed or "dead" file.

▼ Information derived from personal inquiry goes into the brain's "smelter" for refining and assimilation.

▼ Human brains learn best when they are free to assemble randomly supplied information into concepts and programs of action.

▼ The school post office is a good example of an activity that meets five conditions of a brain compatible environment: random input, personal inquiry, learning by doing, magnetic appeal, and free choice.

"A child can learn to talk in three years, even in the jungle without Ph.D. parents! Why should it take ten more years to teach him to *read* the same thing he already knows how to *say*? Kids in ghettos can learn three languages at once, and they can learn to write all kinds of things in secret codes. But the way things are taught in schools produces a situation in which some kids aren't learning to read. Some of you may remember classes where you didn't learn much because of the atrocious way the material was presented."

— Richard Bandler

Frame Eight
Strategies for Greatness

MANY STRATEGIES HAVE BEEN CREATED TO HELP STUDENTS GROW IN individual greatness. When everyone is involved in generating a climate for creative inquiry, there is much enthusiasm about inventing strategies for accomplishing the mission.

The Great Brain Project

The Great Brain project was the first invention of the curriculum-as-servant philosophy of education; it was the first project that aimed to develop the three dimensions of human greatness with parents, teachers, and students acting as full, equal partners aiming for common goals. It is a springboard for the take-charge philosophy of education.

The idea is simple and easy to adopt. Each child is invited to become a "Great Brain" in a subject that interests him or her. This is done through intensive study over a period of weeks or months. When the child is ready, he/she signs up with the teacher to make a Great Brain presentation to classmates, relatives, and friends. Following the presentation, the child's project may be evaluated. The child is then given the appropriate title of "specialist," "expert," "mastermind," or "genius."

The following outline shows activities that can be used to accomplish each of the goals of the mission:

Activities to Develop Inquiry

1. Each student is to select a topic to study for several weeks until he/she becomes a Great Brain on that topic.

2. The student creates a list of questions that guide the search for information, adding to the list as he/she probes deeper into the subject.

3. The student performs hands-on investigations whenever possible.

4. The student reads everything available about the topic, interviews authorities, writes letters, visits on-site locations, analyzes, compares, and ponders.

5. The student keeps a record of findings.

6. The student is taught library skills and is given time to use the library to read, study, and plan.

7. After acquiring all the information desired, the student produces a creative product of original thinking.

Activities to Develop Interaction:

1. The student's parents and other adult friends are invited to become partners with the school in helping the student become a Great Brain.

2. The student interviews authorities and discusses the topic with others.

3. Families discuss and engage in activities that center around the topic.

4. The student prepares and gives a Great Brain recital before an audience of classmates, family, friends, relatives, and other invited guests.

5. The student answers questions from the audience.

"Instruction begins when you, the teacher, learn from the learner; put yourself in his place so that you may understand what he learns and the way he understands it."

— Kierkegaard

Activities to Develop Identity:

1. The project may be evaluated and the student may then be given the title "specialist," "expert," "mastermind," or "genius."

2. The principal formally presents the student with a Great Brain badge to wear.

3. The student's accomplishment is announced over the school public address system.

4. Names of Great Brain achievers are published in school newsletters.

5. A picture is taken and placed on the Great Brain honor roll.

6. A Great Brain award certificate, such as the one below, is presented:

E.M. WHITESIDES ELEMENTARY SCHOOL

GREAT BRAIN AWARD

In recognition of outstanding accomplishment,

this award is presented to

_____

who has earned the title _____

in the area of _____

| _____ | _____ | _____ |
| TEACHER | DATE | PRINCIPAL |

To initiate the project, each child who chooses to become a Great Brain carries home an official entry blank:

The Great Brain Project
Official Entry Blank

On this _____ day of _____ , 199 ___ , I, _____

do hereby enroll in the **Great Brain Project** of _____

School. With my parents' help I have chosen the subject

_____

to study in great depth until I feel qualified and prepared to give a presentation to my friends, relatives, and classmates.

I agree to:

1. Prepare a list of stimulating questions with which to guide my research.

2. Study diligently at school, at home, and in the community.

3. Keep a record of my findings and plan an interesting, creative way to share my new knowledge with others.

4. Let my teacher know when I am ready to make a Great Brain presentation.

I understand that diligent participation in this project may qualify me for a Great Brain award on one of four levels:

| Specialist | Expert | Mastermind | Genius |

It will also entitle me to membership in the Great Brain Club.

I/We the parent(s) of _____ do agree to become partners with my/our child and the school to assist him/her in the chosen quest.

_____   _____
Student's Signature   Parent's Signature

The child and the parents receive one of the following lists of guidelines:

Great Brain Project guidelines for intermediate and middle-school students and their parents:

Steps

1. **Survey**: Do a survey and list several subjects that you may be interested in studying in depth.

2. **Select**: With parents' help, if possible, choose the subject that is most appealing and offers the most promise of new discoveries.

3. **Question**: Make a list of questions you would like to learn about your chosen subject. Keep adding to the list as you dig deeper and deeper.

4. **Study**: Gather information about your subject. Search in all possible places (libraries, newspapers, magazines, television, interviews with authorities, etc.) over a period of at least two months. Read everything you can get your hands on.

5. **Notes:** Keep a record in a notebook of the interesting things you learn as you study and ponder your subject. Do not copy the author's words. Make notes in your own words. Tell some of your own ideas.

6. **Bibliography**: Keep a careful record of where you find each piece of interesting information.

7. **Organize**: Make an outline by assembling ideas into major groupings.

8. **Create**: Develop an original product (story, poem, art, etc.) to reflect your own thinking.

9. **Plan**: Make a plan for sharing your new knowledge with parents, friends, and classmates.

10. **A-V Aids**: Make or collect audio/visual aids (pictures, posters, objects, etc.) to use in the presentation.

11. **Practice**: Give your presentation to family members in a loud clear voice and in your own words. Hear suggestions for im-

provement and try again as many times as necessary.

12. **Preview-Schedule**: Show your work to your teacher so that he/she can check your work and arrange a time for your presentation.

Guidelines for primary or intermediate students:

How to Become a Great Brain

1. **Choose a Topic:**

   You can be smarter than anyone in the whole school, a Great Brain, on any subject you choose. All around you there are ordinary, common things waiting for something new to be discovered about them. Choose one of these for an exciting adventure in learning. Submit an official entry blank to your teacher so he/she will know what topic you will be working on.

2. **Build questions:**

   ▼ Write down all the "facts" that you think you already know about your subject.

   ▼ Make a list of all the things you would like to learn about your subject. Ask questions that start with words such as: "what," "how," "why," "where," "when," "who," and "which."

   ▼ Keep adding to your list of questions while you carry out your investigation.

3. **Conduct an Investigation**

   ▼ Study with your eyes. Observe with all your might. **Look! Look! Look!** Examine carefully.

   ▼ Count, weigh, measure, compare, and classify.

   ▼ Draw and paint pictures of your subject.

   ▼ **Read** everything you can find or have an adult read to you, if material is difficult.

   ▼ Interview authorities.

   ▼ Write for information.

▼ Perform experiments.

▼ Write down answers to your questions and other interesting things you learn about your subject.

4. **Imagine, Create, Invent**

   After filling your mind with information about your subject, use your own ideas to create or invent an original product — a story, a poem, a work of art, a piece of music, a construction, etc.

5. **Prepare and Share**

   Think of a creative, interesting way to share your Great Brain knowledge with your class, relatives, and friends. Take time to carefully prepare visual aids, a speech, or other ways to share that will hold the interest of your audience.

   Practice giving your presentation until you feel confident.

   Sign up with your teacher for a date to make a Great Brain presentation. Do your best.

There are many ways to create interest in Great Brain activity. We found the following story to be an outstanding example of what can be done if we will only open our eyes and explore the amazing world around us. As the story will show, we are limited only by our lack of wonder and imagination. The story can be read to older students but should be told to younger children.

A Great Brain Story

How to discover where your interests lie and how to gather relevant information — the question of where to begin — is illustrated in this story told by Marion Hanks:

An obscure spinster woman insisted that she never had a chance. She muttered these words to Dr. Louis Agassiz, a distinguished naturalist, after one of his lectures in London. In response to her complaint, he replied, "Do you say, madam, you never had a chance? What do you do?"

"I am single and help my sister run a boardinghouse."

"What do you do?" he asked.

"I skin potatoes and chop onions."

He said, "Madam, where do you sit during these interesting but homely duties?"

"On the bottom step of the kitchen stairs."

"Where do your feet rest?"

"On the glazed brick."

"What is glazed brick?"

"I don't know, sir."

He said, "How long have you been sitting there?"

She said, "Fifteen years."

"Madam, here is my personal card," said Dr. Agassiz. "Would you kindly write me a letter concerning the nature of a glazed brick?"

She took him seriously. She went home and explored the dictionary and discovered that a brick was a piece of baked clay. That definition seemed too simple to send to Dr. Agassiz, so after the dishes were washed, she went to the library and in an encyclopedia read that glazed brick is vitrified kaolin and hydrous aluminum silicate. She didn't know what that meant, but she was curious to find out. She took the word vitrified and read all she could about it. Then she visited museums. She moved out of the basement of her life and into a new world on the wings of vitrified. And having started, she took the word hydrous, studied geology, and went back in her studies to a time when the world was covered in clay beds. One afternoon she went to a brickyard, where she found out about the history of more than 120 kinds of bricks and tiles and why there have to be so many. She sat down and wrote thirty-six pages on the subject of glazed brick and tile.

Back came a letter from Dr. Agassiz: "Dear Madam, this is the best article I have ever seen on the subject. If you will kindly change the three words marked with asterisks, I will have it published and pay you for it."

A short time later there came a letter that brought $250, and penciled on the bottom of the letter was this query: "What was under those bricks?" She had learned the value of time and answered with a single word: "Ants." He wrote back and said, "Tell me about the ants."

She began to study ants. She found there were between eighteen hundred and twenty-five hundred different kinds. There are ants so tiny you could put three head-to-head on a pin and have standing room left over for other ants; ants an inch long that march in solid armies half a mile wide, driving everything ahead of them; ants that are blind; ants that get wings on the afternoon of the day they die; ants that build anthills so tiny that you can cover one with a silver thimble; peasant ants that keep cows to milk and that then deliver the fresh milk to other ants in the colony.

After much reading, microscopic work, and deep study, the spinster sat down and wrote Dr. Agassiz 360 pages on the subject. He published the book and sent her the money, and using her earnings she went to visit all the lands she had dreams of visiting.

As you hear this story, do you feel that all of us are sitting with our feet on pieces of vitrified kaolin and hydrous aluminum silicate — with ants under them?

When a child is ready to make a presentation he/she may choose to send invitations to friends, relatives, and others after arranging for a time and place with the teacher(s).

A child's self-concept (identity) is enhanced when he/she accomplishes a difficult task and is recognized for it. This is the purpose of giving Great Brain titles. The titles listed below were chosen to represent five ascending levels of accomplishment.

First level — *Amateur:* A person who is just beginning to learn about a topic.

Second level — *Specialist:* A person who specializes in a particular field of study.

Third level — *Expert:* A person who is very skilled or highly trained and informed in a special field of study.

Fourth level — *Mastermind:* A person with great intelligence in a particular field who is skillful in teaching and directing others.

Fifth level — *Genius:* A person with a great mental capacity and inventive ability in a particular field of study.

The child's work can be evaluated informally by the teacher or measured against a specific set of tasks to be completed by the child.

It is critical that evaluation be kept lighthearted and flexible. Students should not, in any way, be led into competing with one another.

To avoid the problems that can arise, some schools have elected to dispense with external evaluations except when they are requested by the student. Others allow the student and his or her parents to decide the level of attainment. The important point is to always allow the possibility of additional growth. A child may choose to become a "specialist" in one topic, an "expert" in another, and a "mastermind" or "genius" in another, depending on the degree to which the topic captures his/her interest and/or matches the child's unique intelligence profile. Later the child may choose to return to a particular topic for further study. The different levels of accomplishment can be very challenging and motivating as students discover there are different degrees of knowledge and that great accomplishment is the result of hard, enjoyable work.

Some teachers have developed "sticker" booklets for accomplishing each step on the guidelines so that students can know in advance what is expected of them at each level for a particular grade. This provides the benefit of motivating those who need external prodding along each step of the way. Care must be exercised, however, to prevent Great Brain inquiry from taking on the flavor of the deadly "research paper," which turns students away very quickly. It is better to allow individual creative rambling than to overwhelm students at the beginning with a long list of expectations.

On the following page is a sample instrument for evaluating the work of those who want this service:

Great Brain Evaluation

For _____

	Points	Specialist 1	Expert 2	Mastermind 4	Genius 8
Gathering Knowledge					
1. **Questions**					
Quantity					
Quality					
2. **Recording Information**					
Quantity					
Quality					
3. **Reading**					
(Bibliography)					
4. **Other Resources**					
(Interviews, Museums, etc.)					
5. **Creative Product(s) of Original Thinking**					
Presentation					
6. **Loud and Clear**					
7. **Own Words**					
8. **Expression**					
9. **Enthusiasm**					
10. **Holds Audience**					
11. **Visuals**					
12. **Effort**					
13. **Fielding Questions**					
Total Points					

Specialist	10 – 20 points
Expert	21 – 50 points
Mastermind	51 – 100 points
Genius	101 – 120 points

Badges

On the day following each child's presentation a respected adult — a teacher, parent, the principal, or an expert that the child may have interviewed — goes to the classroom and formally presents the student with a Great Brain badge to wear. The badge presenter sincerely acknowledges the child's accomplishment and invites everyone to enthusiastically cheer and applaud.

Various designs are used for the badges in different schools. Below are a few examples:

We have found that next to Great Brain T-shirts, the badges are the most highly coveted symbol of a child's accomplishment. Those that emphasize the child's name seem to do the best job of nurturing an identity of greatness.

You can obtain badge-making apparatus from various companies, make badges by hand, or hand letter on name tags such as those available at most office supply stores.

Photographs

Children swell with pride when their names and pictures appear on the Great Brain Honor Roll in the main hall of the school. Individual close-ups are best, but if funds are limited, you can take groups of up to four children at a time and cut out the individual heads. Thirty-five mm film purchased and developed at large department stores is generally the least expensive.

In a rapidly growing number of schools, hundreds of children from kindergarten through middle grades are working on Great Brain projects. The invitation for children to become Great Brains has a magic effect. By the time a child has made his/her first Great Brain presentation he/she realizes, "My growth is my responsibility and I can accomplish almost anything!" When a school provides the right climate, and once a child gets a taste of free-wheeling, brakes-off inquiry, there is no stopping him/her. The winning attitude becomes part of his/her life.

Some schools have allowed brief, two-month periods of Great Brain inquiry, but the program seems to work best when it is an ongoing, year-long process.

The Great Brain Fair

Children who have completed projects look forward to displaying their wares, accomplishments, and knowledge in a Great Brain fair where each child sets up a booth and stands available to answer questions and expound his/her knowledge to visitors. The fair can be held during the day for students and in the evening for parents.

To further the development of identity, each booth should have a large sign with the student's name, title, and topic on prominent display:

Examples:

SUSAN JONES Expert – Civil War	**RANDY THOMPSON** Great Brain – Whales

Such a sign indicates that we are highlighting the student more than his/her topic.

When children give presentations they should be reminded to save their materials for the Great Brain fair.

The Great Brain program is most quickly launched when it is introduced to parents and students in a general meeting. Don't get discouraged if it seems to go slowly at first. Remember that students need to be offered time daily to study and work on their projects in classrooms, libraries, ships, art centers, science labs, etc. Several weeks should lapse before the first presentation. The process will gather momentum if children's efforts are supported and recognized.

The Great Brain program is one example of the take-charge philosophy of education. Teachers can use this successful program to practice aiming for true goals — the central needs of the human heart. Once it becomes a habit, many other exciting programs will emerge. When one begins to think like a take-charge teacher, great creative power is unleashed with which to develop ways to accomplish the goals.

In my experience with students learning through self-initiated, personal inquiry, achievement is clearly evident in the results. Of hundreds of projects I have seen, I shall relate only a few: Allison, a fourth-grade student, decided to study the workings of the state legislature. She and her mother contacted a state senator and asked for his cooperation in helping the child learn about her chosen topic. This very busy man was so impressed with Allison's enthusiasm and eagerness to learn that he arranged for her to visit the floor of the state senate while it was in session, took her on a tour of the capitol building, and explained how bills become law. As part of her report, Allison showed a video she had made of herself interviewing the senator and of her tour of the capitol.

After studying dinosaurs for several weeks, Kimberly, a fifth grader, composed lyrics and music for a delightful dinosaur song, which she expertly played on the piano and sang as part of her outstanding presentation.

Justin, an energetic six-year-old, demonstrated an amazing knowledge of trucks as he explained the many uses of a great variety of them, including tow trucks, dump trucks, cement trucks, delivery vans, tankers, and eighteen-wheel transports. Justin's original drawing of a large diesel truck with all of the parts labeled was magnificent, as was his collection of toy trucks.

Justin's nine-year old brother, Jason, did an extensive study of the moon with a telescope he had purchased with money earned by selling Christmas cards door to door. In his presentation, Jason demonstrated his telescope and showed many original drawings of different phases of the moon.

The Great Brain presentations help the students realize that they can become brilliant in nearly any endeavor they choose, and thus become a special contributor to society.

"The mind is not a vessel to be filled, but a lamp to be lighted."

— Anonymous

Shining Stars

Another program that aims to identify and develop individual intelligences is described in the following letter:

Dear Parents,

We are pleased to invite all parents and students to become involved in a second phase of education for human greatness — the Shining Stars program. Those who have been involved in the Great Brain project know that education for greatness is a different approach to education in which parents become full partners with the school to develop student greatness. In the Shining Stars program, parents or other mentors such as neighbors or grandparents coach a child in the development of a talent— polishing the talent until it "shines" and the child feels confident to perform before an audience. The child then performs his/her talent for his class or grade level. The child repeats this process as often as time will allow, continually adding to his/her repertoire of shining talents.

The accompanying sheet contains a partial list of talent opportunities from which to choose.

Beginning next month each class or grade level will sponsor talent shows for the Shining Stars to display their talents.

Thanks for your great support with our projects for growth.

Sincerely,

Staff

Shining Stars Possibilities

Arts

painting, oil, water, acrylics
drawing
whittling
carving
sculpting
making ceramics
making puppets
kite-making
paper sculpting
wood constructions
papier-mâché
photography
movie making
video production

Writing

stories
plays
poems
essays
shadow plays
skits

Crafts

cross-stitch
sewing
knitting
crochet
embroidery
quilting
tatting
weaving
textile paintings
cooking
model building
handyman
mechanics

Dramatics

giving humorous readings
telling stories
debating
acting
giving speeches
reciting poetry
being an emcee
performing skits
performing magic tricks

Dancing

ballet
tap
clogging
creative
mime

Misc.

detective
finger math, Chisenbop
pet training
equestrian
checkers, chess

Hobbies

_____

_____

_____

_____

_____

Musical

singing solo
singing duet
quartet, barbershop
instrument playing
homemade instruments
band

Physical

aerobics
juggling
sprinting
distance running
tightrope walking
high jumping
wrestling
weight training
playing basketball
arm wrestling
frisbee throwing
basketball shooting,
    dribbling
long jumping
rope jumping
dart throwing
cheerleading
trick bicycle riding
marble shooting
baton
drill
archery
gymnastics
balance
running

This list is not intended to be final. Please feel free to add any talents we may have overlooked.

The Shining Stars program is the second full partnership program with students, parents, and teachers working together. Parents can share their talents and coach individuals or small groups. This program can be great fun and will grow as students, parents, and teachers see the possibilities for helping each student develop his/her unique repertoire of talents. With the right kind of support and encouragement every child can shine in something.

Weekly talent shows can be held with small group audiences from which "stars" can be nominated to perform for a monthly gathering of a larger group. Two or three times each year those who have worked hard to become "Shining Stars" can perform for the whole school and/or community. A continuing investigation of the list will allow each child to explore a broad range of talents.

The Shining Stars and Great Brain programs often go hand in hand. A student can become a Shining Star in playing a musical instrument and a Great Brain on sound, how the ear works, or a great musician or composer. A student can work individually or with a small group, such as a barbershop quartet or a band, using homemade instruments.

Another option for the Shining Stars program is to give recognition in the form of badges, pictures, certificates, ribbons, etc., similar to those described in the Great Brain program. Formal evaluation for ranking should be avoided, however, unless it is specifically requested by the student.

Challenge Education

Another strategy that leaves responsibility for learning with the student is a big brother to the Great Brain project. It is a strategy for high school students called Challenge Education. In this program, developed by Maurice Gibbons, a high school student spends most of the high school years preparing to make an elaborate presentation to friends, relatives, and classmates to prove that he/she is ready to enter the adult world and be a valuable participant in society. Gibbons suggests that schools should help students prepare to meet five basic challenges:

1. **Adventure:** a challenge to the student's daring, endurance, and skill in an unfamiliar environment.

2. **Creativity:** a challenge to explore, cultivate, and express his or her own imagination in some aesthetically pleasing form.

3. **Service:** a challenge to identify a human need for assistance and provide it; to express caring without expectation of reward.

4. **Practical Skill:** a challenge to explore a utilitarian activity, to learn the knowledge and skills necessary to work in that field, and to produce something of use.

5. **Logical Inquiry:** a challenge to explore curiosity, to formulate a question or problem of personal importance, and to pursue an answer or solution systematically and, wherever appropriate, by investigation.

"Man ultimately decides for himself! And in the end, education must be education toward the ability to decide."

— Viktor Frankl

Challege Education is another strategy that helps students to develop the three dimensions of human greatness. Gibbons shared this exciting vision of a new kind of high school fifteen years ago. At the time it was embraced theoretically by many people, but it has yet to be wholeheartedly accepted and implemented because it is student-centered and not curriculum-centered.

There are myriad other posssible projects and strategies that generate human greatness. A few others to add to the list are:

▼ **School aviary, zoo, or farm**. We developed a zoo to promote firsthand investigation of animals, birds, fish, and insects.

▼ **Industrial arts center and craft facility**. A studio was set up in a large supply room with work benches, easels, and a variety of materials and tools.

▼ **Media center**. Ours was adjacent to the library and contained computers, video equipment, word processors, and a television for viewing videos.

▼ **Field excursions**. The community presented myriad opportunities for firsthand investigation. A survey was taken to determine the sites of interest within a two-mile, a ten-mile, and a twenty-mile radius of the school. Students walked, took public transportation, or rode in the field trip bus.

▼ **Local experts.** Presentations by members of the community were given to share knowledge about their areas of expertise and talents.

▼ **A mentor system**. Students can be grouped with older members of the community or with younger students so they can learn from one another in an exchange.

▼ **Greenhouse**. The one at Hill Field School was part of the aviary — with living trees for the birds to fly around and nest in.

Attitudes

Wherever there is a take-charge philosophy and an atmosphere of independent learning, there are positive effects. Although knowledge and skills blossom, the most dramatic influence has been on students' attitudes — toward the self, learning, and toward others.

These are the kinds of attitudes students learn:

▼ I am responsible for my own learning and behavior.

▼ Satisfying accomplishment is a result of personal effort.

▼ I am a valuable, important person.

▼ Every person is gifted and talented.

▼ Cooperation with others is beneficial to everyone involved.

▼ Learning is a joyous activity.

These attitudes are the beginnings of significant growth in knowledge and skills. Traditional education, with its focus on report cards and achievement tests, is backward in its approach to learning. Significant growth in basic skills seems to follow, not precede, attitude development.

Summary for Frame Eight:

▼ The Great Brain program is an exercise that: nurtures student growth in greatness, helps parents and teachers learn how to be partners, is a model for the curriculum-as-servant philosophy of education, and is a pattern to follow for redesigning education around student-centered goals.

▼ When students are turned loose to learn, with guidance and support from parents and teachers working as partners, they can accomplish amazing things.

▼ Student attitudes about self, others, and about learning, are all enhanced through participation in programs such as those discussed in this chapter.

Summary
The Framework for Redesigning Education

1. Mission: Develop great human beings who are valuable contributors to society.

2. Master Goals:

Identity: Individual intelligences, talents and gifts, confidence, self-esteem, honesty, spirituality, character, and physical fitness.

Interaction: Love, compassion, respect, empathy, communication, and responsible citizenship.

Inquiry: Passion for learning; the ability to acquire, process, and use information to gain knowledge, create understanding, and solve problems.

These master goals are in response to the three central drives of every person: the drive to be an important "somebody" (identity), the drive for warm human relationships (interaction), and the drive for truth and knowledge (inquiry). It is the intense, continuous concentration on the mission and master goals by students, parents, and teachers that makes the remaining design frames possible:

3. E. T. Partnerships: Parents and teachers work *equally* and *together* as full partners to help students grow in the three dimensions of greatness.

4. A Take-Charge Philosophy: Teachers, parents, and students use curricula as a means rather than an end, as a servant rather than a master.

5. Evaluation of Greatness: Evaluation is used to assess student growth in identity, interaction, and inquiry.

6. Multiple Intelligences: Each student is an individual with a unique set of "intelligences" to be developed — not a single IQ.

7. Brain Based: Parents and teachers stimulate students to activate the full power of their minds through personal inquiry.

8. Strategies: Strategies are the how-to steps that emerge when students, parents, and teachers hold a clear vision of the mission and master goals constantly in mind.

Conclusion

EDUCATION FOR HUMAN GREATNESS IS A STUDENT-CENTERED FRAMEWORK for redesigning education that makes a clean break with the traditional, curriculum-centered, assembly-line model. It has been my intention that this guide will give parents and educators everywhere the courage to build a new system of education based on the framework that is provided, in which each of the frames represents one component of a comprehensive whole. Where there are flaws I hope they will be overshadowed by the greater ideas. All that remains now is for you, the reader, to consider this philosophy and find a teacher, parent, or school administrator to be your partner in the exciting enterprise of building a new system of education for your community — one that stimulates the growth of the "great brains" who live there.

Valuable Resources:
Tools for Implementation

The following resources are invaluable if you are educating for human greatness:

Whole-Brain Learning and Imagery

Bagley, Michael T. *200 Ways of Using Imagery in the Classroom: A Guide for Developing the Imagination and Creativity.* Monroe, N.Y.: Trillium Press, 1987.

Campbell, Don G., and Chris Boyd Brewer. *Rhythms of Learning: Creative Tools for Academic Development.* Tucson, Ariz.: Zephyr Press, 1991.

Galyean, Beverly-Colleene. *Mind Sight: Learning Through Imagery.* Berkeley, Calif.: Center for Integrative Learning, 1984.

Jensen, Eric. *Super-Teaching: Master Strategies for Building Student Success.* Delmar, Calif.: Turning Point for Teachers, 1988.

Margulies, Nancy. *Mapping Inner Space.* Tucson, Ariz.: Zephyr Press, 1991.

Mason, Kathy. *Going Beyond Words: The Art and Practice of Visual Thinking.* Tucson, Ariz.: Zephyr Press, 1991.

McCarthy, Bernice. *The 4-MAT System: Teaching to Learning Styles with Right/Left Mode Techniques.* Barrington, Ill.: Excel, Inc., 1987.

McKisson, Micki. *Chrysalis: Nurturing Creative and Independent Thought in Children.* Tucson, Ariz.: Zephyr Press, 1983.

Rose, Laura. *Picture This: Teaching Reading Through Visualization.* Tucson, Ariz.: Zephyr Press, 1991.

Vitale, Barbara Meister. *Unicorns Are Real: A Right-Brained Approach to Learning.* Rolling Hills Estates, Calif.: Jalmar Press, 1982.

Whole Language

Bergstrom and Bergstrom. *All the Best Contests for Kids 1990-1991: Hundreds of Contests and Opportunities That Test Your Skill and Challenge Your Brain.* Berkeley, Calif.: Ten Speed Press, 1990.

Borg, Mary. *Writing Your Life: An Easy-to-Follow Guide to Writing an Autobiography.* Fort Collins, Colo.: Cottonwood Press, 1989.

Colgin, Mary Lou. *One Potato, Two Potato, Three Potato, Four.* Mt. Rainier, Md.: Gryphon House, 1989.

Draze, Diane. *Literature Companion.* San Luis Obispo, Calif.: Dandy Lion Publications, 1986.

Feldman, David. *Who Put the Butter in Butterfly? And Other Fearless Investigations into Our Illogical Language.* New York: Harper and Row, 1989.

Foley and Bagley. *Suppose the Wolf Were an Octopus: A Guide to Creative Questioning.* Monroe, N.Y.: Trillium Press, 1988.

Harmin, Merrill. *SPUNJZ: Language Arts Activities for Self-Awareness.* Tucson, Ariz.: Zephyr Press, 1992.

Hovis and Domin. *Word for Word: Creative Thinking Projects for Building Vocabulary.* Tucson, Ariz.: Zephyr Press, 1990.

Koch and Farrell. *Talking to the Sun: An Illustrated Anthology of Poems for Young People.* New York: Metropolitan Museum of Art, 1985.

Maguel and Guadalupi. *Dictionary of Imaginary Places*. Orlando, Fla.: Harcourt Brace Jovanovich, Publishers, 1987.

Polette, Nancy. *Whole Language in Action: Teaching with Children's Literature*. O'Fallon, Mo.: Book Lures, Inc., 1984.

Raines and Candy. *Story Stretchers: Activities to Expand Children's Favorite Books*. Mt. Rainier, Md.: Gryphon House, Inc., 1989.

Personal Development

Adderholdt-Elliott, Miriam. *Perfectionism: What's Bad About Being Too Good*. Minneapolis, Minn.: Free Spirit Publishing, 1987.

Benzwie, Teresa. *A Moving Experience: Dance for Lovers of Children and the Child Within*. Tucson, Ariz.: Zephyr Press, 1988.

Bingham, Edmondson, and Stryker. *Choices: A Teen Women's Journal for Self-Awareness and Personal Planning*. Santa Barbara, Calif.: Advocacy Press, 1987.

Borba and Borba. *Self-Esteem: A Classroom Affair: 101 Ways to Help Children Like Themselves*. San Francisco, Calif.: Harper Collins, 1982.

Brigman and Earley. *Peer Helping: A Training Guide*. Portland, Maine: Weston Walch, 1990.

Chichak and Heron. *Games Children Should Play: Sequential Lessons for Teaching Communication Skills*. Glenview, Ill.: Good Year Books, 1980.

Cole, Jim. *Filtering People: Understanding and Confronting Our Prejudices*. Philadelphia, Pa.: New Society Publishers, 1990.

Devencenzi and Pendergast. *Belonging: Self and Social Discovery for Children of All Ages*. San Luis Obispo, Calif.: Belonging, 1988.

Dinkmeyer and Losoucy. *The Encouragement Book: Becoming a Positive Person*. New York: Prentice Hall, 1980.

Drew, Naomi. *Learning the Skills of Peacemaking: An Activity Guide for Elementary-Age Children*. Rolling Hills Estates, Calif.: Jalmar Press, 1987.

Gibbons, Maurice. *How to Become an Expert: Discover, Research, and Build a Project in Your Chosen Field*. Tucson, Ariz.: Zephyr Press, 1991.

Gibbs, Jeanne. *Tribes: A Process for Social Development and Co-operative Learning*. Santa Rosa, Calif.: Center Source Publishers, 1987.

Hartline, Jo Ellen. *Me!? A Curriculum for Teaching Self-Esteem Through an Interest Center*. Tucson, Ariz.: Zephyr Press, 1990.

Henderson, Kathy. *What Would We Do Without You? A Guide to Volunteer Activities for Kids*. White Hall, Va.: Betterway Publications, 1990.

Hopkins and Winters, eds. *Discover the World: Empowering Children to Value Themselves, Others and the Earth*. Philadelphia, Pa.: New Society Publishers, 1990.

Kramer, Patricia. *The Dynamics of Relationships: A Guide for Developing Self-Esteem and Social Skills for Preteens, Teens, and Young Adults*. Kensington, Md.: Equal Partners, 1990.

Kreidler, William J. *Creative Conflict Resolution: More than 200 Activities for Keeping Peace in the Classroom*. Glenview, Ill.: Good Year Books, 1984.

Schniedewind and Davidson. *Cooperative Learning, Cooperative Lives: A Sourcebook of Learning Activities for Building a Peaceful World*. Dubuque, Iowa: Wm. C. Brown Co., 1987.

Ungame, The. Anaheim, Calif.: Talicor Inc., 1987.

Wade, Rahima Carol. *Joining Hands: From Personal to Planetary Friendship in the Primary Classroom*. Tucson, Ariz.: Zephyr Press, 1991.

Thinking Skills

Bellanca and Fogarty. *Blueprints for Thinking in the Cooperative Classroom*. Palatine, Ill.: Skylight Publishing, 1990.

Binker, Paul. *Critical Thinking Handbooks: A Guide for Remodeling Lesson Plans in Language Arts, Social Studies, and Science*. Rohnert Park, Calif.: Foundation for Critical Thinking, Sonoma State University, 1990.

Chaffee, John. *Thinking Critically*. Boston, Mass.: Houghton Mifflin, 1985.

DeBono, Edward. *DeBono's Thinking Course*. New York: Facts on File, 1985.

_____. *Six Thinking Hats.* Boston, Mass.: Little, Brown, 1985.

Hawley and Hawley. *Teacher's Handbook of Practical Strategies for Teaching Thinking in the Classroom.* Amherst, Mass.: ERA Press, 1987.

Lipman, Mathew. *Philosophy for Children.* Montclair, N.J.: First Mountain Foundation.

Meeker, Mary. *SOI Sourcebooks.* El Segundo, Calif.: SOI Institute, 1979.

Thornburg and Thornburg. *Thinkers' Toolbox: A Practical and Easy Approach to Creative Thinking.* Palo Alto, Calif.: Dale Seymour Publications, 1989.

Tyler, Sydney. *Just Think* (series). Montana, Calif.: Thomas Geale Publications.

Udall, Anne J., and Joan E. Daniels. *Creating the Thoughtful Classroom: Strategies to Promote Student Thinking.* Tucson, Ariz.: Zephyr Press, 1991.

Arts and Humanities

Black, Kaye. *Kidvid: Fun-damentals of Video Instruction.* Tucson, Ariz.: Zephyr Press, 1989.

Edgar and Carr. *Worldways: Bringing the World into the Classroom.* Reading, Mass.: Addison-Wesley, 1987.

Hollingsworth and Hollingsworth. *Smart Art: Learning to Classify and Criticize Art.* Tucson, Ariz.: Zephyr Press, 1989.

Images. St. Louis, Mo.: Milliken Publishing Co.

Jaffe, Charlotte. *Cu Ra' Tor Express: An Excursion in Art Appreciation.* Tucson, Ariz.: Zephyr Press, revised 1989.

Longstreet, Stephen. *Magic Trumpets: The Story of Jazz for Young People.* Tucson, Ariz.: Zephyr Press, 1989.

Mack and Christine. *The Tribal Design: The Many Faces of Cultural Art.* Tucson, Ariz.: Crizmac, 1988.

Patton, Sally. *Alphabetics: A History of Our Alphabet,* rev. ed. Tucson, Ariz.: Zephyr Press, 1989.

_____. *Musicians,* rev. ed. Tucson, Ariz.: Zephyr Press, 1992.

_____. *Reflections on Women in Monarchies and Democracies,* rev. ed. Tucson, Ariz.: Zephyr Press, 1991.

Patton and Madigan. *Philosophers,* rev. ed. Tucson, Ariz.: Zephyr Press, 1989.

Patton and Maletis. *Artists.* Tucson, Ariz.: Zephyr Press, 1976.

_____. *Inventors,* rev. ed. Tucson, Ariz.: Zephyr Press, 1989.

Patton and Maxon. *Architexture: A Shelter Word.* Tucson, Ariz.: Zephyr Press, 1989.

Ryan, Margaret W. *Cultural Journeys: 84 Art and Social Science Activities From Around the World.* Holmes Beach, Fla.: Learning Publications, Inc., 1990.

Ventura, Piero. *Great Composers.* New York: G. P. Putnam's Sons, 1989.

_____. *Great Painters.* New York: G. P. Putnam's Sons, 1984.

Math Appreciation

Benzwie, Teresa. *Math: A Moving Experience.* 1981. (Available through Zephyr Press, Tucson, Ariz.)

Burns, Marilyn. *A Collection of Math Lessons.* New Rochelle, N.Y.: The Math Solutions Publications, 1987.

_____. *The Book of Think: Or How to Solve a Problem Twice Your Size.* The Math Solutions Publications, 1976.

Davidson, Neil, ed. *Cooperative Learning in Mathematics: A Handbook for Teachers.* Reading, Mass.: Addison-Wesley, 1990.

Erickson, Tom. *Get It Together: Math Problems for Groups.* Berkeley, Calif.: Univ. of California Press, 1989.

Stenmark, Thompson, and Cossey. *Family Math.* Berkeley, Calif.: Univ. of California, 1986.

Wahl, Mark. *A Mathematical Mystery Tour: Higher-Thinking Math Tasks.* Tucson, Ariz.: Zephyr Press, 1988.

Science

Baeckler, Virginia. *Storytime Science.* Hopewell, N.J.: Sources, 1986.

Barkman, Robert. *Coaching Science Stars: Pep Talk and Play Book for Real-World Problem Solving.* Tucson, Ariz.: Zephyr Press, 1991.

Bonnet and Deen. *Earth Science: 49 Science Fair Projects*. Blue Ridge Summit, Pa.: Tab Books, 1990.

Grier, Katherine. *Discover*. Reading, Mass.: Addison-Wesley, 1989.

Hassard, Jack. *Science Experiences: Cooperative Learning and the Teaching of Science*. Reading, Mass.: Addison-Wesley, 1990.

Holzinger, Philip R. *The House of Science*. John Wiley & Sons, 1990.

MacRae-Campbell, McKisson, and Campbell. *Our Only Earth series: Endangered Species: Their Struggle to Survive; Our Divided World: Poverty, Hunger & Overpopulation; Our Troubled Skies; The Future of Our Tropical Rainforests; The Ocean Crisis; War: The Global Battlefield*. Tucson, Ariz.: Zephyr Press, 1990.

_____. *The Energy Crisis*. Tucson, Ariz.: Zephyr Press, 1992.

MaKower and Fenichal. *The Air and Space Catalog: The Complete Sourcebook to Everything in the Universe*. New York: Vintage Books, 1989.

Ontario Science Centre. *Scienceworks: 65 Experiments That Introduce the Fun and Wonder of Science*. Reading, Mass.: Addison-Wesley, 1984.

_____. *Sportsworks: More than 50 Fun Activities That Explore the Science of Sport*. Reading, Mass.: Addison-Wesley, 1989.

Wolfe, Connie. *Search: A Research Guide for Science Fairs and Independent Study*. Tucson, Ariz.: Zephyr Press, 1988.

Organizations to Write to:

ACCESS: A Security Information Service
1730 M St., N.W., Ste 605
Washington, D.C. 20036
202/785-6630
Helps concerned citizens find the best resources available — across the political spectrum — on issues like arms control, foreign policy, regional conflicts, and the economic aspects of global security. Offers an inquiry service, speaker referral service, briefing papers, and guides to resources and foundations.

Council for the Advancement of Citizenship
1724 Massachusetts Ave., N.W.
Washington, D.D. 20036
202/857-0580
A consortium of 85 national and regional organizations dedicated to the teaching of citizenship; CAC has an array of clearinghouse services and programs.

American Newspaper Publishers Association Foundation
P.O. Box 17407 Dulles Airport
Washington, D.C. 20041
Has information on contact persons at newspapers in your region that offer programs on using newspapers for educational purposes. Write Betty Sullivan at the above address.

Constitutional Rights Foundation
601 S. Kingsley Dr.
Los Angeles, CA 90005
213/487-5590
Provides technical assistance, teacher training, and curriculum materials in the areas of law-related education, youth leadership, and youth community service programs. Contact Todd Clark or Kathleen Kirby.

National Issues Forums
100 Commons Dr.
Dayton, OH 45459-2777
Offers materials and study guides for the examination of important public issues by students or adults. Also offers a "Participation in Government" curriculum for schools.

A Presidential Classroom for Young Americans
441 N. Lee St.
Alexandria, VA 22314-2346
1-800-441-6533
Students attending the "Presidential Classroom" in Washington, D.C., learn about government firsthand through an array of seminars with political leaders.

Bibliography

Armstrong, Thomas. *In Their Own Way: Discovering and Encouraging Your Child's Personal Learning Style*. Los Angeles, Calif.: J. P. Tarcher, 1987.

Barbar, Benjamin R. "Public Talk and Civic Action: Education for Participation in a Strong Democracy." *Social Education* 53 (October 1989): 356-356, 370.

Beery, Keith. *The Guts to Grow*. San Rafael, Calif.: Dimensions, 1974.

_____. *Ohana: Hawaii's Greatest Gift.* Honolulu, Hawaii: The Respect Institute, 1986.

Boyer, Ernest L. "Civic Education for Responsible Citizens." *Educational Leadership* 48, 3 (November 1990): 4-7.

Brandt, Ron. "The Search for Solutions." *Educational Leadership*. October 1985.

Buzan, Tony. *Use Both Sides of Your Brain*. New York: Dutton, 1974.

Cherry, Godwin, and Staples. *Is the Left Brain Always Right? A Guide to Whole Child Development*. Belmont, Calif.: Fearon Teacher Aids, 1989.

Colfax, David, and Micki Colfax. *Home Schooling for Excellence: How to Take Charge of Your Child's Education*. New York: Warner Books, 1988.

DeMoss, Nancy Leigh, ed. *The Rebirth of America*. Philadelphia, Pa.: Arthur S. DeMoss Foundation, 1986.

Diamond, Marian Cleeve. *Enriching Heredity: The Impact of the Environment on the Anatomy of the Brain*. New York: The Free Press, 1988.

Dronka, Pamela, ed. *ASCD Update*. March 1984.

Edwards, B. *Drawing on the Right Side of the Brain: A Course in Enhancing Creativity and Artistic Confidence*. Los Angeles: J. P. Tarcher, 1979.

Feldenkrais, Moshe. *Awareness Through Movement*. New York: Harper and Row, 1972.

Fox, Patricia L. *Reading as a Whole Brain Function*. The Reading Teacher, October 1979.

Gallwey, W. T. *Inner Tennis*. New York: Random House, 1976.

Gardner, Howard. *Chinese Clues to the Dilemma of Contemporary Education*. New York: Basic Books, 1989.

Gardner, Howard. *The Frames of Mind: Theory of Multiple Intelligences*. New York: Basic Books, 1985.

Geschwind, Norman. "Language and the Brain," *Scientific American,* April 1972.

Gibbons, Maurice. *The Walkabout Papers*. Vancouver: EduServ, 1990.

Goertzel and Goertzel. *Cradles of Eminence*. Boston, Mass.: Little, Brown & Co., Inc., 1962.

Guilford, J. P. "Intellectual Factors in Productive Thinking." *Productive Thinking in Education*. Washington, D.C.: National Education Association, 1968.

Hanks, Marion D. *The Gift of Self*. Salt Lake City, Utah: Bookcraft, 1977.

Hart, Leslie A. *Human Brain and Human Learning*. New York: Longman, 1983.

Investing in Our Children. New York: Committee for Economic Development, Research, and Policy, 1985.

Kline, Peter. *The Everyday Genius: Restoring Children's Natural Joy of Learning — and Yours Too.* Arlington, Va.: Great Ocean Publishers, 1988.

Lawrence, Gordon. *People Types & Tiger Stripes: A Practical Guide to Learning Styles,* rev. ed. Gainesville, Fla.: Center for Applications of Psychological Type, 1982.

Lewis, C. S. *Mere Christianity.* New York: Macmillan, 1972.

Maltz, Maxwell. *Psycho-Cybernetics.* New York: Prentice Hall, 1960.

Marzello, Jean, and Janice Lloyd. *Learning Through Play.* New York: Harper and Row, 1972.

Medvedeff, Eugene. *New Dimensions in Learning.* Iowa City, Iowa: Westinghouse Learning Corp., 1975.

Miller, Maureen. *To Share with Your Children.* Niles, Ill.: Argus Communications, 1978.

Miller, Ron. *New Directions in Education: Selections from Holistic Education Review.* Brandon, Vt.: Holistic Education Press, 1991.

Miller, Ron, ed. *What Are Schools For? Holistic Education in American Culture.* Brandon, Vt.: Holistic Education Press, 1990.

Montessori, Maria. *The Absorbent Mind.* New York: Dell Publishing, 1967.

——————. *The Discovery of the Child.* Notre Dame, Ind.: Fides Publishers, 1967.

Naisbitt, John, and Patricia Aburdene. *Reinventing the Corporation.* New York: Warner Books, 1985.

Neve, Charmaine Della, Leslie A. Hart, and Edgar C. Thomas. "Huge Learning Jumps Show Potency of Brain-Based Instruction." *Kappan,* October 1986.

Odiorne, George S. *Management and the Activity Trap.* New York: Harper & Row, 1974.

Paivio, Allen. *Imagery and Verbal Processes.* New York: Holt, Rinehart, and Winston, 1971.

People for the American Way. *Democracy's Next Generation: A Study of Youth and Teachers.* Washington, D.C.: People for the American Way, 1989.

Purkey, William W., and John J. Schmidt et al. *Invitational Learning for Counseling and Development*. Ann Arbor, Mich.: ERIC Counseling and Personal Services Clearinghouse, 1990.

Read, Herbert. *Education Through Art*. New York: Pantheon, 1974.

Restak, R. M. *The Brain: The Last Frontier*. Garden City, N.J.: Doubleday, 1979.

Samples, Bob. *Openmind/Wholemind: Parenting and Teaching Tomorrow's Children Today*. Rolling Hills Estates, Calif.: Jalmar Press, 1987.

Smith, Frank. *Essays into Literacy*. London: Heinemann, 1983.

Staley, Frederick A. *Outdoor Educaton for the Whole Child*. Dubuque, Iowa: Kendall/Hunt, 1979.

Taylor, Calvin. "A High-Tech High-Touch Concept of Creativity— with Its Complexity Made Simple for Wide Adoptability." *Frontiers of Creative Research: Beyond the Basics*. Edited by Scott Isaksen. New York: Bearly Limited Press, 1987.

_____. "Cultivating Simultaneous Student Growth in Both Multiple Creative Talents and Knowledge." *Systems and Models for Developing Programs for the Gifted and Talented*. Edited by Joseph Renzulli. Mansfield, Conn.: Creative Learning Press, Inc., 1987.

Walters, Joseph M., and Howard Gardner. "The Development and Education of Intelligences." *Essays on Intellect*. Edited by Francis R. Link. Washington, D.C.: Association for Supervision and Curriculum Development, 1985.

Wedemeyer, Avaril, and Joyce Cejka. *Learning Games for Exceptional Children*. Denver, Colo.: Love Publishing, 1971.

Williams, Roger J. *You Are Extra-Ordinary*. New York: Random House, 1967.

Wilson, Robert. "The Structure of the Intellect." *Productive Thinking in Education*. Washington, D.C.: National Education Association, 1968.

Wlodkowski and Jaynes. *Eager to Learn: Helping Children Become Motivated and Love Learning*. San Francisco: Jossey-Bass, 1990.

If you have developed your own ideas of human greatness with which to guide parents and teachers, have modified the elements I discussed, or have developed strategies for helping students grow in the dimensions of greatness, you are invited to send your work to the publisher so that this framework can be improved. Write to Zephyr Press, P.O. Box 13448, Tucson, AZ 85732-3448.

SEVEN PATHWAYS OF LEARNING

Teaching Students and Parents about Multiple Intelligences
by David Lazear

David Lazear dedicates his new book to helping students tap into their full learning potential.

Encourage your students to pass through four distinct levels of thinking about intelligence. Each step encompasses a wider spiral of understanding. Make effective use of the seven intelligences by going through these levels—

- Tacit—becoming aware of individual capabilities
- Aware—strengthening personal intelligence
- Strategic—knowing how and when to use each type of intelligence
- Reflective—integrating multiple intelligences into everyday life

Incorporate thinking about intelligences into your classroom. Show students how to master classroom assignments and to enrich lifelong learning.

For teachers of K-Adult.
302 pages, 8 1/2" x 11", softbound.
ZB45-W—$30

To order, write or call—
Zephyr Press
P.O. Box 13448-W
Tucson, Arizona 85732-3448
Phone—(602) 322-5090
FAX—(602) 323-9402

You can also request a free copy of our current catalog showing other learning materials that foster whole-brain learning, creative thinking, and self-awareness.

DOORWAYS TO LEARNING

A Model for Developing the Brain's Full Potential
by Peter Majoy

Open *Doorways to Learning* to discover a model for teaching and learning based on the function of the whole brain.

Capitalize on the real experiences of students by respecting each individual learning style. Use this model to effectively traverse ability groups, age groups, and socio-economic boundaries.

Find the theory behind each of the seven doorways of learning. You'll have lots of activities you can adapt to any curricular area.

You'll find methods to—

- Promote a blend of challenge and calmness
- Produce firsthand experiences, the most effective way to learn
- Encourage the exchange of information among all learners
- Incorporate movement into special settings, such as exams
- And much more

Using this model will make a difference in your classroom! You'll find the model easy to adapt to your teaching styles. On a broader level *Doorways to Learning* can help you effect school reform and restructure!

For teachers of K-Adult.
256 pages, 7" x 10", softbound.
ZB41-W—$25